CHANGE YOUR MIND

TO

CHANGE YOUR LIFE!

MITCH HORTON

WESTBOW
PRESS®
A DIVISION OF THOMAS NELSON
& ZONDERVAN

WestBow Press books may be ordered through booksellers or by contacting:

WestBow Press
A Division of Thomas Nelson & Zondervan
1663 Liberty Drive
Bloomington, IN 47403
www.westbowpress.com
844-714-3454

ISBN: 978-1-6642-3934-0 (sc)
ISBN: 978-1-6642-3935-7 (hc)
ISBN: 978-1-6642-3933-3 (e)

Library of Congress Control Number: 2021913307

Print information available on the last page.

WestBow Press rev. date: 7/22/2021

CONTENTS

PREFACE

This book is a result of my personal search for ways to curb the tendencies I had as a young Christian, when I allowed my mind to wander into areas of my past life that hindered my walk with God. Now, more than forty years later, the principles that I mention here have transformed the way I think and live. I have been able to overcome so many negative traits by simply following through daily with seeking to keep my mental focus on how God my Father sees me in His Word.

Habits are changed by replacing them with other habits. As you read this book, ask yourself a few introspective questions and seek to replace your negative mental habits.

Here are some questions to ask yourself:

- Am I controlling my thoughts, or are my thoughts controlling me?
- Do current events frequently remind me of things in my past that have hurt or hindered my life?
- Do I deliberately seek to control what I think about?
- Do I allow my thoughts to meander randomly from one subject to another without stopping them?
- Do I take time daily to meditate on scriptures from the Bible that can encourage and help me?

- Do I look for specific scriptures that can help me focus on the positive truths of who I am in Christ?
- Do I meditate on them regularly?

As you read the following chapters, seek to apply the truth to your own life. Don't give up if you stumble and fail. We all do. The key is to get up and apply the simple principles you read here. The result will be a transformed life. I hope you enjoy reading this book and are changed by its truths.

CHAPTER ONE

FOUR THINGS TO KNOW ABOUT CONTROLLING YOUR THOUGHTS

The mind is under tremendous assault today. In this information age, it is possible to have no alone time mentally. Most people don't realize that as goes the mind, so goes the life. As a Christian, if you are going to have a strong walk with God, you must learn to harness your thoughts and not allow them to go helter-skelter.

In this series of lessons, we will look at how Satan uses thoughts as roads into our lives. We will look at steps you can begin to take to renew your mind with God's Word. We will discuss the importance of meditation in the Word. And then we will end by looking at how our personal belief systems can be changed through meditation in the Word of God.

Satan seeks to intoxicate us mentally.

The mind of the average person today is blinded by Satan. Notice 2 Corinthians 4:4 (NLT):

> Satan, who is the god of this world, has blinded the minds of those who don't believe. They are unable to

see the glorious light of the Good News. They don't
understand this message about the glory of Christ,
who is the exact likeness of God.

Satan distorts our perceptions of God, ourselves, and others,
deemphasizes the important, and magnifies the trivial. He makes
wrong look right, good look bad, and so forth. The prophet Isaiah
says it clearly in Isaiah 5:20 (NLT):

What sorrow for those who say that evil is good and
good is evil, that dark is light and light is dark, that
bitter is sweet and sweet is bitter.

These sinister thought patterns come from God's archenemy, Satan.

The New Testament reveals to us that Satan has a scheme, a plan, a
path, and a method, or you could call it a road of attack into every
life. That road into each life is the road of thought.

We read in 1 Peter 5:8 (NKJV), "Be sober, be vigilant; because your
adversary the devil walks about like a roaring lion, seeking whom
he may devour." The word *sober* here is *nepho,* and according to
Vine's Complete Expository Dictionary, it means "to be free from
the influence of intoxicants." In context, it is speaking of mental
intoxicants. Alcoholic beverages cause physical intoxication. And a
person who is physically intoxicated will think, say, and do things
that are outlandish and out of character.

Similarly, a person who is mentally intoxicated by worry, doubt,
fear, self-centeredness, and the desires of the flesh and surrounding
culture will do things *spiritually* that are out of character for a
believer! Satan seeks to intoxicate us mentally. So, here in 1 Peter,
we are encouraged to practice mental self-control.

First Peter 5:8 also encourages us to be *vigilant.* To be vigilant means
"to be ever on your guard." The rest of the verse tells us that Satan

walks about as a lion on the prowl, looking for a person who is not watching and is not aware that he or she is in a spiritual battle. We must never let our mental defenses down. Satan is looking for the person who is not aware that danger looms with every wayward thought. All of us must stand against Satan's schemes of mental intoxication.

Satan enters a life through the roadway of thought.

We read in Ephesians 6:11–12 (NKJV),

> Put on the whole armor of God, that you may be able to stand against the *wiles* of the devil. For we do not wrestle against flesh and blood, but against principalities, against powers, against the rulers of the darkness of this age, against spiritual hosts of wickedness in the heavenly places.

The Greek word *wiles* in this verse is *methodeia,* and it literally means "with a road." The idea here is that Satan travels down a certain path, or a certain road, to gain entrance into a human life. The road Satan travels into a life is the road of *thoughts.* I think you can begin to see the importance of watching and guarding our thoughts. Satan is ever seeking to lead us onto a detour from the path or road of life that God has for us.

If we can maintain control of our thinking and not let it get out of hand, then we can keep Satan and his subtle schemes out of our lives.

Four Things to Know about Controlling the Mind

In this chapter, we are going to look at four points that give understanding to how we function spiritually and the important part our minds play in our spiritual development.

1. You are a spirit, you have a soul, and you live in a body.
2. The new birth transforms the spirit nature.

3. The mind must be renewed for the spirit to be free.
4. The mind resists change! You have to force it to obey God!

1. You are a spirit, you have a soul, and you live in a body.

God has given us His viewpoint of how we function as spiritual beings in a physical world. Notice 1 Thessalonians 5:23 (NLT):

> Now may the God of peace make you holy in every way, and may your whole spirit and soul and body be kept blameless until our Lord Jesus Christ comes again.

We are spiritual beings in physical bodies. The combination of the spirit of humans coming from God at creation into a physical body creates a living soul. Let's look at each part of us mentioned here in a simple way.

Spirit

Our spirit is the part of our person that relates to God. God created us to fellowship with Him. He is a spirit being. Notice John 4:24 (AMPC), "God is a Spirit (a spiritual Being) and those who worship Him must worship Him in spirit and in truth (reality)." And since we are created to fellowship with God spiritually, then we likewise are spiritual beings in physical bodies. Job 32:8 (NKJV) says, "But there is a spirit in man, and the breath of the Almighty gives him understanding."

Our spirit nature has a voice the Bible calls "conscience." We sometimes refer to this voice of the spirit nature as intuition, an inner knowing, or a gut sense. All these terms refer to the voice of the spirit nature of man. The voice of the spirit of man is deeper than thought and comes from the deepest, most spiritual part of our person.

Soul

Our soul is the part of our person that relates to the world around us. The predominant voice of the soul is reasoning. The soul is made up of three parts: intellect, emotion, and will. So *thinking, feeling,* and *willing* come from the soul of a person.

Spirit and soul are often spoken of as the same thing. A person may mention that so many souls were saved in an evangelistic outreach. Or we may sing about God saving our soul. But if you examine the Bible carefully, you will see that spirit and soul can be divided. And if they can be divided, then they are not the same thing.

To see this, read with me Hebrews 4:12 (NLT).

> For the word of God is alive and powerful. It is sharper than the sharpest two-edged sword, cutting between soul and spirit, between joint and marrow. It exposes our innermost thoughts and desires.

The introduction by God of the spirit of man into a human body created the soul. We read in Genesis 2:7 (NLT), "Then the Lord God formed the man from the dust of the ground. He breathed the breath of life into the man's nostrils, and the man became a living person."

Body

I call our body the *earth suit* that we live in. An astronaut has a space suit. The astronauts who go on space walks outside the space station circling the earth must be dressed for the environment of outer space. Our bodies dress our spirit natures for earth's environment. When we die, we shed our earth suit, and our spirit and soul combined, our inner man, goes into eternity.

The primary voice of the body is the five senses. We learn all we know from hearing, seeing, smelling, tasting, and touching. The sixth sense would be a spiritual sense we call conscience or intuition. It comes from our spirit and gives us information it receives from the spirit realm, which cannot be contacted by the physical body and its senses.

When Adam was first created, his spirit flowed in unity with God. His soul was in harmony with his spirit and was the servant of his spiritual life. His body was in harmony with the earth, for God created our bodies from dirt (Genesis 2:7 NLT). His entire being flowed in complete agreement and harmony, each part complementing the other.

The following picture shows, in a simplistic way, our spirit, soul, and body and how they function:

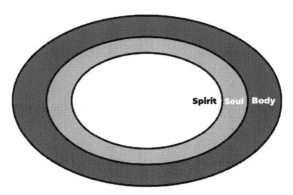

Spirit Soul Body

Spirit - King
Soul - Servant
Body - Slave

Soul	**Spirit**	**Body**
Reason & Emotion	Conscience	Feelings
	2 Corinthians 5:17 - New nature	
Mind, Emotions, and Will	Galatians 5:22-23	Home of the 5 Senses
Romans 12:2		Hearing, Taste, Touch, Smell,
Thoughts, Emotions, Motivation		Sight
"Self Seat"	Love	
	Joy	
	Peace	
	Longsuffering	
	Gentleness	
	Goodness	
	Faith	
	Meekness	
	Self-Control	
	The Holy Spirit	

2. The new birth transforms the spirit nature.

We are sinners by nature. In fact, the Bible calls the nature of a human without God "spiritual death." Spiritual death is separation from God. Notice Romans 5:12 (NLT). When Adam sinned, sin entered the world. Adam's sin brought death, so death spread to everyone, for everyone sinned.

Jeremiah tells us the heart of man, his spirit nature, is corrupt. Jeremiah 17:9 (NLT) says, "The human heart is the most deceitful of all things, and desperately wicked. Who really knows how bad it is?" All of us have sinned and are corrupt at heart. Listen to Jesus. "For from the heart come evil thoughts, murder, adultery, all sexual immorality, theft, lying, and slander." Matthew 15:19 (NLT) Paul tells us that all of us have sinned. "For everyone has sinned; we all fall short of God's glorious standard" (Romans 3:23 NLT).

Jesus, speaking to a religious Jewish leader, said that we must be born again, or born from above, to go to heaven!

> There was a man named Nicodemus, a Jewish religious leader, who was a Pharisee. After dark one evening, he came to speak with Jesus. "Rabbi," he said, we all know that God has sent you to teach us. Your miraculous signs are evidence that God is with you. Jesus replied, "I tell you the truth, unless you are born again, you cannot see the Kingdom of God." (John 3:1–3 NLT)

The new birth is the rebirth of the dead human spirit from spiritual death to spiritual life. When we are born again, our spiritual nature changes from death to life. "Yet we can be assured that we have been translated from spiritual death into spiritual life because we love the family of believers. A loveless life remains spiritually dead." (1 John 3:14 TPT)

This new birth of the spirit nature is mentioned by both Paul and Peter:

> Therefore if anyone is in Christ [that is, grafted in, joined to Him by faith in Him as Savior], he is a new creature [reborn and renewed by the Holy Spirit]; the old things [the previous moral and spiritual condition] have passed away. Behold, new things have come [because spiritual awakening brings a new life]. (2 Corinthians 5:17 AMP)

> For you have been born again [that is, reborn from above—spiritually transformed, renewed, and set apart for His purpose] not of seed which is perishable but [from that which is] imperishable and immortal, that is, through the living and everlasting word of God. (1 Peter 1:23 AMP)

Prior to making Jesus Lord and being born again, our spiritual nature is corrupted by sin. Notice the effects of this inward spiritual corruption:

> When you follow the desires of your sinful nature, the results are very clear: sexual immorality, impurity, lustful pleasures, idolatry, sorcery, hostility, quarreling, jealousy, outbursts of anger, selfish ambition, dissension, division, envy, drunkenness, wild parties, and other sins like these. Let me tell you again, as I have before, that anyone living that sort of life will not inherit the Kingdom of God. (Galatians 5:19–21 NLT)

After the new birth, God deposits His very life and nature within us. We pass from spiritual death to spiritual life, and the fruit of our lifestyle changes:

> But the Holy Spirit produces this kind of fruit in our lives: love, joy, peace, patience, kindness, goodness, faithfulness, gentleness, and self-control. There is no law against these things! Those who belong to Christ Jesus have nailed the passions and desires of their sinful nature to his cross and crucified them there. (Galatians 5:22–24 NLT)

We are like newborn babies with no past after we are born again. But there is another process of change that we must allow for this new nature to rule our lives.

3. The mind must be renewed for the spirit to be free.

When we repent of our personal sin and give our hearts and wills to Jesus Christ, we are inwardly transformed, but our minds remain embedded with the residue from our sinful nature.

The apostle Paul mentions this when writing to Christians in Rome. Read this carefully:

> I urge you therefore, brothers, by the mercies of God, that you present your bodies as a living sacrifice, holy, and acceptable to God, which is your reasonable service of worship. Do not be conformed to this world, but be transformed by the renewing of your mind, that you may prove what is the good and acceptable and perfect will of God. (Romans 12:1–2 MEV)

Paul urges these Christians to willingly relinquish control of their bodies to God, and in this way they can worship Him. He then tells them that their thinking must also change. Here are several translations of Romans 12:2 that will emphasize the importance of renewing our minds as Christians:

Don't copy the behavior and customs of this world, but let God transform you into a new person by changing the way you think. Then you will learn to know God's will for you, which is good and pleasing and perfect. (Romans 12:2 NLT)

I therefore beg of you, please, brethren, through the instrumentality of the aforementioned mercies of God, by a once-for-all presentation to place your bodies at the disposal of God, a sacrifice, a living one, a holy one, well-pleasing, your rational, sacred service, rational, in that this service is performed by the exercise of the mind. (Romans 12:1 Wuest—The New Testament: An Expanded Translation)

Stop imitating the ideals and opinions of the culture around you, but be inwardly transformed by the Holy Spirit through a total reformation of how you think. This will empower you to discern God's will as you live a beautiful life, satisfying and perfect in his eyes. (Romans 12:2 TPT)

Don't let the world around you squeeze you into its own mould, but let God re-mould your minds from within, so that you may prove in practice that the plan of God for you is good, meets all his demands and moves towards the goal of true maturity. (Romans 12:2 PHILLIPS)

Our lives will go the direction of our thoughts. The mind is the pivot point between spiritual living and carnal living for the Christian. Paul makes it clear here that what we do with our minds every day will determine what kind of life we will live.

For most people today, some form of media controls what they think from the time they get up in the morning until the time they go to bed. Christians today would do well to heed Paul's instructions here. The reason for the loose living among believers today is because of the failure to heed Paul's teaching to clean up our thought patterns.

Mind renewal is a lifelong venture. It never ceases, and it is one of our more difficult challenges as a Christian.

4. The mind resists change. You have to force it to obey God!

> For those whose lives are according to the flesh think about the things of the flesh, but those whose lives are according to the Spirit, about the things of the Spirit. For the mind-set of the flesh is death, but the mind-set of the Spirit is life and peace. For the mind-set of the flesh is hostile to God because it does not submit itself to God's law, for it is unable to do so. Those whose lives are in the flesh are unable to please God. (Romans 8:5–8 HCSB)

This verse in Romans 8 emphasizes that whatever we think about rules our conduct. If I put my thoughts on carnal, fleshly things, I will live a carnal, fleshly life. If I focus my mind on spiritual things, then I will live a spiritually oriented life. I choose what my life looks like by choosing what dominates my daily thoughts.

This verse also brings out a shocking thought that our minds are actively hostile to God. That means that if my mind is left unattended, it will naturally lead me away from God.

Here are a few other translations of Romans 8:7 to make the point very clear. The natural mind unaided by the Holy Spirit will not submit to God's ways:

In fact, the mind-set focused on the flesh fights God's plan and refuses to submit to his direction, because it cannot! (Romans 8:7 TPT)

The mind of the flesh [with its sinful pursuits] is *actively hostile to God*. It does not submit itself to God's law, since it cannot. (Romans 8:7 AMP)

For the mind-set of the flesh is hostile to God because it does not submit itself to God's law, for it is unable to do so. (Romans 8:7 HCSB Free)

The soul has a life of its own. It makes the unreal seem real and strictly opposes any movement to unseat its control!

Many years ago, when I was in my twenties and early thirties, I had a sense of rejection and inferiority that shadowed me at times. It was a by-product of my early childhood. When I turned thirty, I pioneered a church in a small rural town. I would preach my heart out on Sundays and then on Mondays have strong thoughts and feelings that many of the people in my new church just did not like me. This persisted week after week, and I knew I just could not continue to be effective in ministry with these thoughts and feelings hounding me.

So I decided to test these strong thoughts that produced strong emotions of rejection by calling various people in my congregation that my mind told me did not like me. After I preached on Sunday, I would make the calls midmorning on Monday. I would engage several people in conversation just to see what kind of responses and what kind of tone the conversation had with them. To my amazement, not one of them was thinking what my mind and emotions told me about them. All of them were very grateful that I was their pastor and that I took the time to call.

This taught me a very valuable lesson in my early years that has helped me so much in life. And it was such a shock to discover this.

Here is what I found out. My mind, or I could say our minds, have a life of their own. They are hostile to God and have the ability to create their own reality that isn't really true. So that means that my mind can hijack my life throughout the day if I am not diligent to control it! And it can make me think and feel that things are a certain way when they really are not! This has helped me immeasurably in walking with the Lord and particularly in walking by faith.

We must learn to control what we think, and to tell our minds what God says about the various areas of life. And we must learn to refuse to allow our minds to hijack our lives!

Thirty Symptoms of a Renewed Mind and Thirty Symptoms of an Unrenewed Mind

Check yourself against the following lists of items that reveal a mind that has been transformed by God's Word and a mind that still has a life of its own. Some of the items seem to overlap, and to a degree, they may. But they are showing similar things from different angles. In chapter 2, I will address how to begin the process of mind renewal.

Thirty Symptoms of an Unrenewed Mind

1. Little interest in the Word
2. Little understanding of who you are in Christ
3. Thinking only of the negatives in your life
4. Lack of joy
5. Lack of personal freedom and liberty to be yourself
6. Constantly dwelling on past thoughts, feelings, and actions
7. Lack of godly love and forgiveness
8. Fear of openness and honesty
9. Impure thinking and living
10. Lack of humility and submission—stubbornness
11. Weak faith in God and His Word

12. More concerned with what people think than with what God thinks and wills
13. Motivated by feelings more than God's Word
14. Fear of financial failure
15. Fear of sickness and disease; obsession with symptoms
16. Fear of God and others
17. Fear of closeness and intimacy with others
18. Fear of exposure, of letting people know who you really are
19. Inferiority
20. Loneliness
21. Easily hurt and offended, overly sensitive
22. Inability to accept criticism
23. Fault finding: reading bad motives into what others do
24. Pessimistic attitude
25. Sinful physical habits
26. Self-pity
27. Inability to give and receive love
28. Constant critical demeanor toward spouse
29. Gossip
30. Looking for negative thoughts and traits in others

Thirty Symptoms of a Renewed Mind

1. Genuine love and concern for others
2. Joy
3. Inward peace
4. Patience with people
5. Patience in circumstances
6. Seeing the best in others
7. Sense of fulfillment
8. Sense of acceptance with God
9. Lack of personal inferiority
10. Knowing your place in Christ
11. Forgiveness
12. Unconditional love

13. Purity in thought and life
14. Ability to be comfortable revealing yourself to others
15. Ability to enjoy close relationships
16. Thoughts of health and healing
17. Knowing you are materially provided for
18. Optimism even in tough circumstances
19. Believing the best of others
20. Faith in the Word over feelings
21. Confidence in God
22. Proper sense of personal boundaries
23. Freedom to be open and honest
24. Treating others with kindness
25. Lack of worry
26. Using words that bless and heal
27. Honesty
28. Keeping your word
29. Doing your best in all you do
30. A thankful attitude, even when life is hard

Action Points

1. Can you identify the thoughts you have that are providing a road for Satan to attack you?
2. Can you differentiate within your spirit, your soul, and your body?
3. How do you know that you've been born again?
4. Do you have symptoms of an unrenewed mind?

CHAPTER TWO

FOUR STEPS TO MIND RENEWAL AND LIFE CHANGE

Over the years, I have taken notes and archived them as I have read various books. Here are a few quotes about the mind that I archived from the 1980s. I have read them over and over during the ensuing years, and they have urged me to keep my mind free and clear.

Mind Quotes

You can't keep a bird from flying over your head. But you can keep him from building a nest in your hair! (Kenneth Hagin)

A man's life will be as the character of his thoughts. If he thinks evil, he will be evil. If he thinks holy, he will be holy. His outward life will be as his inner impulse is. (John G. Lake)

You live the way you think—so what the mind feeds upon becomes the most influential force of your life. (Tim Lahaye)

> The devil knows that if he can capture your thought life, he has won a mighty victory over you ... I come across people everywhere I go who are held bound by deceptive conditions, and these conditions have come about simply because they have allowed the devil to make their mind the place of his stronghold. (Smith Wigglesworth)

> You cannot have spiritual power without purity of mind. (Lester Sumrall)

Keep in mind that our minds tend to have lives of their own. As I mentioned previously, the mind ruled by the flesh has a hostile attitude toward God, and unless we choose to control it, it will lead us away from fellowship with Him and into allegiance with our surrounding culture. "In fact, the mind-set focused on the flesh fights God's plan and refuses to submit to his direction, because it cannot!" (Romans 8:7 TPT).

As a believer, our spirit name has been transformed from darkness to light and from sin to righteousness. When old thoughts return, they are only an echo of the old self we were. They are a former, practiced, habitual way of thinking from our past, before-Christ life.

To help guide us into a new way of living and thinking, I submit to you four steps to mind renewal:

1. Locate the wrong thoughts.

Mental Ruts

We all have mental ruts (like the grooves on a vinyl record). These ruts are formed from thought patterns that are created from years of living and experiencing certain things in our past. These ruts are also created from thought patterns that are built into us in infancy and childhood.

A rut is an automatic way of thinking about yourself and life that you naturally default back to under pressure. We *all* have mental ruts. We must choose to identify them, challenge them, and then change them. What are your mental ruts?

Years ago, before paved roads, the roads were dirt, and ruts would form in the dirt roads. There was sometimes a sign posted on a long road: *Choose your ruts carefully; you'll be in them for seven miles!*

When I was young, we lived off of the main road and had to drive down a dirt road to get to our house. We had some neighbors who also accessed their home from the dirt road but lived fairly close to the main road. When we turned onto the dirt road near their house, there was a huge hump in the middle of the dirt road created where the neighbors' tires had carved out ruts in the dirt road as they turned onto their property.

When I began to drive, my dad would always encourage me to drive down our long dirt road and never drive on the same portion of the road. He told me to zigzag a bit so that ruts would not form on the road to our house like the neighbors had formed on the road near their house.

Our minds like what is familiar. It's the easiest way. It takes less effort. But over time, mental ruts can form, just like they can on a dirt road. Mental ruts can also run deep and be challenging to get rid of.

My Mental Ruts

The mental ruts from my childhood included thoughts like, *Nobody likes you; nobody cares; you're not like everyone else; there is something wrong with you.* Where did those ruts come from? Well, first of all, my dad cut my brown, curly hair at home. I never went to a real barber until I was fourteen or so, when I began to earn a few dollars for some off-the-grid work here and there. I never liked my hair. To me, it was unmanageable and looked unkempt.

Secondly, my dad bought my clothes about two to three sizes too large. I had to grow into them. As a result, I pulled my belt into almost the last loop available, just to keep my pants from falling down! Then, my pants were rolled up two to three times at the cuff because they were too long. To top off all of this, my feet grew out to a size thirteen by the fifth grade, before I grew taller. To me, I looked like a clown! And that thinking produced some of my personal ruts. My mental image of me produced thoughts of rejection. I rejected myself and then expected others to reject me too.

Other mental ruts developed as I got older. My dad was an exemplary carpenter and an all-around repairman. He was mechanically inclined and could repair most anything that broke around our home. He would often enlist my help to remove a bolt, or to tighten a screw. Invariably, as a novice helper, I would wrench the head off the bolt by tightening it too tightly. Or I would damage the head of the screw so that no screwdriver would fit. And my dad would see it and comment, "Mitch, do you think you can do anything right?" My dad was joking in his own way, but my mind took those words and twisted them into *I can't do anything right.*

Then I had a strange thing happen at a Halloween carnival put on by a neighboring Methodist church. Among the games and activities on Halloween night, they also had a palm reader, who would read your palm and tell you your future. (How dumb can churches be sometimes!) Of course, that sounded exciting to my friends and me. So, when I had my palm read, the person told me that my *lifeline* was short and that I was destined to die young. I stopped enjoying the carnival and left not long after that. And my developing mind played those words over and over in the ensuing weeks, months, and years. I developed a belief from that experience that I would die of some terrible disease or accident and that I would never live to be an older person.

Lastly, my mental ruts from my childhood background formed a belief that I was not worthy to have nice things. I bought the cheapest cars, the cheapest shirts, pants, shoes, and so on. I never owned more than one pair of dress shoes, one pair of school shoes or work shoes, and then one pair of athletic shoes. As I got a little older and even after marriage, I felt guilty when buying clothing that was more than just a few dollars!

As I got older and God began to bless me a little more financially, I had to face the mental barriers that kept me from doing better with material things in life. My mental ruts were beginning to bring limits into my life that I needed to remove.

Many people have mental ruts from their past that limit them so much in life. And the sad thing is that many people are not even aware that they have the wrong thinking. What about you? Do you have mental ruts that keep you from progressing in areas of your life? These mental barriers can change with God's help! To change them, we must begin to control what we think about.

Do You Control Your Thinking throughout the Day?

When I came to Jesus at almost eighteen years old, I began to read my Bible voraciously! As I read, the ruts that had formed in my thinking began to be revealed.

As I read the Word, I began to know that my mental ruts were wrong. As I read, I began to see that I was a new creature in Christ, that old things in my life had passed away, and that all things have become new. Second Corinthians 5:17 (NLT) reads, "This means that anyone who belongs to Christ has become a new person. The old life is gone; a new life has begun!"

I began to see that I was the righteousness of God in Jesus. I begin to see that I could stand before God without condemnation and inferiority. Second Corinthians 5:21 (NLT) reveals, "For God made Christ, who never sinned, to be the offering for our sin, so that we could be made right with God through Christ."

I began to see that God loved me and accepted me:

> Just as He chose us in Him before the foundation of the world, that we should be holy and without blame before Him in love, having predestined us to adoption as sons by Jesus Christ to Himself, according to the good pleasure of His will, to the praise of the glory of His grace, by which He made us accepted in the Beloved. (Ephesians 1:4–6 NKJV)

I found out that Jesus took my sicknesses when He took my sins on the cross:

> That it might be fulfilled which was spoken by Isaiah the prophet, saying: He Himself took our infirmities and bore our sicknesses. (Matthew 8:17 NKJV)

I began to see that God has actually promised us a long life. The Lord says, "I will rescue those who love me. I will protect those who trust in my name. When they call on me, I will answer; I will be with them in trouble. I will rescue and honor them. I will reward them with a long life and give them my salvation" (Psalm 91:14–16 NLT).

I found out that God wanted to meet both our spiritual and material needs. "But seek first the kingdom of God and His righteousness, and all these things shall be added to you" (Matthew 6:33 NKJV).

But my thoughts and feelings ganged up on me. They told me that my life was still of no value and that I was worthless. If I had yielded to my thoughts, I would still be bound today!

But I made the choice to resist the wrong thinking. I knew they were lies! I decided to find scriptures to refute the wrong thoughts.

2. Find scriptures that refute the wrong thinking and feelings.

I found scriptures that refuted the wrong thinking, wrote them on an index card, and stuck it in the front pocket of my shirt. We did not yet have the internet. Cell phones were nonexistent. Everything was written by hand. Today, I would have put these scriptures in the notes section of my mobile phone so I could pull it out and look at them throughout the day.

I found that the Word of God has the power to change your thinking. Notice these scriptures:

> How shall a young man cleanse his way? By taking heed and keeping watch [on himself] according to Your word [conforming his life to it]. (Psalm 119:9 AMPL)

> Your Word have I laid up in my heart, that I might not sin against You. (Psalm 119:11 AMPL)

> His heart pumps God's Word like blood through his veins; his feet are as sure as a cat's. (Psalm 37:31 MSG)

When thoughts came that told me nobody cared, nobody loved me, that I was different from everyone else, and couldn't do anything right, I found a scripture that challenged it and wrote it on a card:

> But, as a matter of fact, it matters very little to me what you, or any man, thinks of me—I don't even value my opinion of myself. For I might be quite ignorant of any fault in myself—but that doesn't justify me before God. My only true judge is the Lord. (1 Corinthians 4:3–4 J. B. Phillips)

When thoughts from my mental ruts came back and told me that I would get sick and die, I found 1 Peter 2:24 (NKJV) and wrote it down and kept it with me:

> Who Himself bore our sins in His own body on the tree, that we, having died to sins, might live for righteousness—by whose stripes you were healed.

When thoughts came and told me that I would die young just like the person said at the Halloween carnival, I found psalm 91 and wrote it on a card to keep with me:

> He shall call upon Me, and I will answer him; I will be with him in trouble; I will deliver him and honor him. With long life I will satisfy him, And show him My salvation. (Psalm 91:15–16 NKJV)

When thoughts came from my ruts and told me that I was not worthy to ever have anything, so don't expect it, I found Luke 12 and wrote it down and kept it with me:

> But seek the kingdom of God, and all these things shall be added to you. Do not fear, little flock, for it is your Father's good pleasure to give you the kingdom. (Luke 12:31–32 NKJV)

3. Catch yourself when thinking and acting on the thoughts.

I learned to say out loud what God said about me throughout my day, and little by little, the ruts in my thinking began to disappear. But I had to be consistent with it. I acknowledged to God that the thoughts had been a stronghold in my life. I asked the Holy Spirit to help me overcome the wrong thinking.

I began to catch myself when the thoughts would return. I acknowledged to the Lord that the thoughts and feelings of inferiority were strong, and I asked Him for grace to overcome them.

I said out loud that I was accepted by God and was loved and favored by Him! I said out loud that I was *not* going to get sick. I said out loud that I was *not* going to die young! I said out loud that I was worthy to be blessed and have things as I sought first the kingdom of God! I confessed out loud what God said about me, and I thanked Him for freeing me from it.

4. Siege the thoughts.

After I found the scriptures and began to refute the wrong thinking about my life, I found that I had to be very persistent. Entrenched thinking does not go away easily. I had to keep watch over my thoughts and emotions and not allow them to rule me. Second Corinthians 4:18 (NKJV) says, "While we do not look at the things which are seen, but at the things which are not seen. For the things which are seen are temporary, but the things which are not seen are eternal." I chose to keep my focus on what God said and not on what I felt. I made a decision to let God's Word rule me and not my carnal thoughts and emotions.

In Eastern culture in Bible days, an enemy army would *siege* a city that had high walls and was impenetrable. They would cut off the supply lines to the city that provided food, water, and materials necessary for life. The inhabitants would be worn down, and then they would breach the walls. It took longer, sometimes years, but the city would be conquered!

I began to siege my wrong thinking. When it appeared, I refused to think the thoughts. I would say out loud what God said about me. I sieged them until they no longer had control.

I have been free for many years from the crushing thoughts and feelings of inferiority that come from fear-based thinking. I have been free for years of thinking that told me that I was going to get sick! I have been free for years from thinking that told me I was going to die young! I have followed this pattern in so many areas of life to become free from thinking that inhibits who I am in Jesus. It works every time.

I encourage you to incorporate the four points we just covered into your life. Challenge the ruts of thinking that hold you back from God's best.

Look at the pattern for freedom from wrong thinking again:

1. Locate the wrong thought.
2. Find scriptures that refute the wrong thinking and feeling and meditate.
3. Catch yourself when thinking and acting on the thoughts.
4. Siege the thoughts.

   It's the Word that can transform our thinking. James 1:21 (NLT) says, "So get rid of all the filth and evil in your lives, and humbly accept the word God has planted in your hearts, for it has the power to save your souls."

Action Points

1. Where do you struggle the most in your thoughts?
2. What are your thinking ruts? Is it guilt? Anxiety? Inferiority? Fear? Pride? Sickness? Fear of death?
3. Ask God to show you the root of your thinking, and then find scriptures that correct what you have been believing.
4. Then get busy saying out loud what you believe every time the thought comes! Siege those ruts!

CHAPTER THREE

MEDITATION ON THE WORD WILL CHANGE YOUR LIFE

If you want to change the way you live, the first step is to change what you are thinking. Thoughts, both realized thoughts that you are aware of and underlying thought patterns that create life context and values, determine the course of life.

I have found that the Word of God is more powerful than thoughts. The Word is transformative. The Word can root wrong thinking out of our minds and can change the underlying thought patterns produced by years of living and interacting with others.

Notice these verses:

> So get rid of all the filth and evil in your lives, and humbly accept the word God has planted in your hearts, for it has the power to save your souls. (James 1:21 NLT)

> Therefore lay aside all filthiness and remaining wickedness and receive with meekness the engrafted word, which is able to save your souls. (James 1:21 MEV)

> For we have the living Word of God, which is full of energy, and it pierces more sharply than a two-edged sword. It will even penetrate to the very core of our being where soul and spirit, bone and marrow meet! It interprets and reveals the true thoughts and secret motives of our hearts. (Hebrews 4:12 TPT)

I found that meditation on the Word is a real key to personal life change. Shortly after I gave my life to Jesus at age eighteen, I found that my mind was hijacking my thinking and keeping me bound to past feelings and a sense of worthlessness.

Thought association, with sights, smells, and sounds, was being used by my mind to keep me aware of what my life had been involved in before I gave my life to Jesus. A smell would take me to a place a few years back. Seeing a person would often remind me of a relationship with someone years before. The grocery store where I worked as a teenager in my late teens played popular music in the background for the shoppers. Those songs reminded me of who I had been and what my life was formerly absorbed with, and it produced feelings of melancholy and pessimism. The thoughts that came with thought association gave me a hopeless sense that I would never change.

I was desperate to find a way to keep my mind from hijacking my spiritual life with Jesus. I would pray when wrong thoughts came, but as soon as I finished praying, the thoughts would come back. Then I tried rebuking the thoughts in the name of Jesus, but the thoughts persisted. I tried to sing and worship to keep the wrong thoughts out, but again, as soon as I stopped the singing and worshipping, these unwanted thoughts flooded my mind.

I was reading one day and found Philippians 4:8 to be a real help as well as a personal challenge. Here are two translations of it:

> And now, dear brothers and sisters, one final thing. Fix your thoughts on what is *true*, and *honorable*, and *right*, and *pure*, and *lovely*, and *admirable*. Think about things that are excellent and worthy of praise. (Philippians 4:8 NLT)

> Finally, brethren, whatsoever things are *true*, whatsoever things are *honest*, whatsoever things are *just*, whatsoever things are *pure*, whatsoever things are *lovely*, whatsoever things are of *good report*; if there be any *virtue*, and if there be any *praise*, think on these things. (Philippians 4:8 KJV)

Finally, out of sheer desperation, I decided to take one scripture each day, write it out on a notecard (no phones or internet back then), and place the notecard in my pocket. I found that my mind would go back into my past, and I wouldn't even realize how long I had been thinking these negative thoughts.

When I realized the wrong thinking, I would take the card out of my pocket, read the scripture on it two or three times, and then think about the scripture. I would let it roll over and over in my mind. I would say it to myself over and over while I worked. To my amazement, the negative thought faded away, and I found a sense of peace that I so wanted.

The practice of filling my idle mental time with meditating on the Word changed what I believed about God, about myself, about my relationship to others, about my life, about my health, about my finances, and literally about everything in my life!

The Bible Encourages Meditation, Not Just Reading

Meditation is thinking more deeply than simply reading. Let me mention again that this is not Eastern religion meditation; nor is it saying a word or mantra over and over; nor is it putting your mind on nothing. True scriptural meditation is focusing on scripture with your mind.

Notice these scriptures that emphasize meditation:

> This Book of the Law shall not depart from your mouth, but you shall *meditate* in it day and night, that you may observe to do according to all that is written in it. For then you will make your way prosperous, and then you will have good success. (Joshua 1:8 NKJV)

> Listen, O Israel! The Lord is our God, the Lord alone. And you must love the Lord your God with all your heart, all your soul, and all your strength. And you must commit yourselves wholeheartedly to these commands that I am giving you today. *Repeat them again and again* to your children. *Talk about them* when you are at home and when you are on the road, when you are going to bed and when you are getting up. Tie them to your hands and wear them on your forehead as reminders. Write them on the doorposts of your house and on your gates. (Deuteronomy 6:4–9 NLT)

> Be angry, and do not sin. *Meditate* within your heart on your bed, and be still. Selah. (Psalm 4:4 NKJV)

> When I remember You on my bed, I *meditate* on You in the night watches. (Psalm 63:6 NKJV)

> I call to remembrance my song in the night; I *meditate* within my heart, And my spirit makes diligent search. (Psalm 77:6 NKJV)

I will also *meditate* on all Your work, and talk of Your deeds. (Psalm 77:12 NKJV)

I will *meditate* on Your precepts, and contemplate Your ways. (Psalm 119:15 NKJV)

Make me understand the way of Your precepts; So shall I *meditate* on Your wonderful works. (Psalm 119:27 NKJV)

My hands also I will lift up to Your commandments, Which I love, And I will *meditate* on Your statutes. (Psalm 119:48 NKJV)

Let the proud be ashamed, For they treated me wrongfully with falsehood; But I will *meditate* on Your precepts. (Psalm 119:78 NKJV)

My eyes are awake through the night watches, That I may *meditate* on Your word. (Psalm 119:148 NKJV)

I remember the days of old; I *meditate* on all Your works; I muse on the work of Your hands. (Psalm 143:5 NKJV)

Blessed is the man Who walks not in the counsel of the ungodly, Nor stands in the path of sinners, Nor sits in the seat of the scornful; But his delight is in the law of the Lord, And in His law he *meditates* day and night. He shall be like a tree Planted by the rivers of water, That brings forth its fruit in its season, Whose leaf also shall not wither; And whatever he does shall prosper. (Psalm 1:1–3 NKJV)

My son, keep my words, And *treasure my commands within you*. Keep my commands and live, And my law as the apple of your eye. Bind them on your fingers; *Write them on the tablet of your heart.* (Proverbs 7:1–3 NKJV)

Oh, how I love Your law! It is my *meditation* all the day. You, through Your commandments, make me wiser than my enemies; For they are ever with me. I have more understanding than all my teachers, For Your testimonies are my meditation. (Psalm 119:97–99 NKJV)

Speaking to one another in psalms and hymns and spiritual songs, singing and making melody in your heart to the Lord. (Ephesians 5:19 NKJV)

Let the word of Christ *dwell in you richly* in all wisdom, teaching and admonishing one another in psalms and hymns and spiritual songs, singing with grace in your hearts to the Lord. (Colossians 3:16 KJV)

The above verses reveal that as you let the Word of God revolve over and over in your mind, the meditation places the Word deep into your heart, your spirit!

Practical Ideas to Meditate on the Word

Scriptural meditation is simply allowing a scripture to revolve over and over in your mind. I want you to notice the definitions from Strong's Exhaustive Concordance of the two main Hebrew words in the Bible for the word *meditate*:

Meditate

Strong's 1897. הגה haga; a primitive root; to murmur (in pleasure or anger); by implication, to ponder:— imagine, meditate, mourn, mutter, roar, speak, study, talk, utter, to moan, growl, muse, devise, plot, to groan

Meditate.

Strong's 7878. שׂיחַ siyah; a primitive root; to ponder, i. e. (by implication) converse (with oneself, and hence, aloud) or (transitively) utter:—commune, complain, declare, meditate, muse, pray, speak, talk (with); to put forth, ponder, sing.

Warren Wiersbe says that "meditation is to the mind and spirit what digestion is to the body." Meditation is like chewing your food. When I was young, I developed a habit of eating too quickly. I can still hear my mom telling me, "Mitch, slow down and chew your food, son!"

When you meditate, you slow down and go over a verse word for word. You think about each word. Start by reading a verse over and over repeatedly. Then emphasize each word one at a time as you read it over and over. This process will cause the Word to drop down into your heart from your head. And that dropping down about a foot from your head to your heart will change how you live your life.

When you meditate, I suggest that you find scriptures that specifically refute the wrong thinking that you are presently experiencing. That way, you are working on a problem that you are dealing with, and you will notice the progress, which can help keep you motivated to continue.

I started meditating in 1976, the year I gave my life to Jesus. I started by saying out loud what the Bible said about me. I would walk back and forth and speak out loud specific scriptures that helped me where I struggled. I would slowly say out loud, "I am a new creature in Christ Jesus; old things are passed away, behold all things are become new" (from 2 Corinthians 5:17 KJV). I would verbalize, "There is therefore now no condemnation to them which are in Christ Jesus, who walk not after the flesh, but after the spirit" (Romans 8:1 KJV). I would repeat Mark 11:24 (KJV) in my thoughts over and over again, "What things soever you desire when you pray, believe that you receive them, and you will have them."

You can meditate by speaking softly out loud or by repeating a scripture over and over in your mind. For decades now, I have practiced meditation, and the effect has been profound.

It changed my personality from fear to faith based. It changed me from having guilt-based thoughts about myself to having a righteousness consciousness.

It changed me from believing the worst to believing the best about others. It changed me from having a poverty, I-don't-have-enough mentality to having a more-than-enough mentality. I would say out loud while meditating, "I have not only enough to meet my needs but enough to give away."

It changed me from being body conscious to spirit conscious. It changed me from being fearful of being sick to having faith that I will remain healthy lifelong. It changed me from thinking that God did not love me to knowing that He loves me as much as He loves His own Son, Jesus!

It changed me from being afraid to do something new to being willing to take a risk and believing that I could do anything God asked me to do! It changed me from being afraid of problems and challenges to knowing that I will overcome every difficulty with God's help!

A Life-Changing Quote from E.W. Kenyon

Here is a quote from E.W. Kenyon that I have had in my files for more than forty years. This quote was a catalyst for me to continue to meditate. This quote validated what I was already doing!

Read this quote from *The Hidden Man* by E.W. Kenyon, p. 53–54:

> The mostly deeply spiritual men and women I know are people who have given much time to meditation. You cannot develop spiritual wisdom without meditation. Joshua 1:8 [KJV] "This book of the law shall not depart out of thy mouth, but thou shalt meditate thereon day and night, that thou mayest observe to do according to all that is written therein: for then thou shalt make thy way prosperous, and then thou shalt have good success" (or deal wisely in the affairs of life). Take time to meditate in the Word. Shut yourself in alone with your own spirit where the clamour of the world of the world is shut out. If you are ambitious to do something worthwhile, I would suggest that you take ten or fifteen minutes for meditation ... learn to do it. In other words, begin the development of your own spirit. You may develop any gift that you wish to. The most important gift that God has given to you is the spirit. It is the development of this spirit that is going to mean more to you than any other thing. The great majority of men do not think. They live in the realm of the senses. The senses have limitations. Your spirit has practically no limitations. You can develop your spirit life until

you dominate circumstances. Your spirit can come into vital union with deity, become a partaker of the Divine nature. That spirit, with God's nature in it, can fellowship with God on terms of absolute equality with God Himself. Do you see your limitless possibilities? Jesus brings you into contact with spiritual things, not mental things. Spiritual things are as real as physical things. Your spirit can come to the point where the things in His Word will become as real to you, and Jesus will become as real to you, as any loved one. You can see the necessity of your taking time to meditate, to get quiet with the Lord. You must take time to sit with His Word and let the Spirit unveil His Word to your spirit. If you will, you will know Him in reality.

Action Points

1. Find scriptures that refute your wrong thinking.
2. Speak them out loud slowly for five to ten minutes a day.
3. Find one scripture each day to put your mind on when mentally idle.

CHAPTER FOUR

HOW YOU CAN CHANGE YOUR PERSONAL BELIEF SYSTEM

We have a system of thinking that is embedded deeply within our minds that controls how we think and respond to life each day. I call it our *personal belief system.* This personal belief system is developed by our interaction with the world. I will come back to this thought later.

After birth, we begin to interact with our environment and learn quickly how to respond to the varying areas of life. We learn by *observation, association,* and *influence.* We watch how others do things, we associate with others and see their responses and attitudes, and we are influenced by others from the moment of birth. And we immediately begin to catalog how to deal with life. Children love to mimic what they see and hear.

By observation, association, and influence, we learn what it means to be loved, valued, and cared for in a family. We learn that we are distinct from others. We learn what *mother* means, what *father* means, what it means to be a boy or a girl. We learn how to communicate and interact on varying levels of life. We learn to value living things over nonliving things.

Some of what we learn has an unhealthy twist to it based on the character faults of our imperfect moms, dads, siblings, and family environments. This distorts our belief system and causes us to believe things about ourselves, others, family, marriage, communication, responses, and a host of other things that hinder us in all sorts of ways in our relationships.

And unless God's Word harnesses and changes what we believe about ourselves and about life that has been distorted by living in an imperfect world, we will continue on as believers and practice many of the hurtful, distorted ways of living that we found in our family upbringing.

An example of how an unchanged belief system will affect our life can be found in God's challenge to Israel about the nations around them that served pagan gods and practiced some really sordid idolatry. Notice God's challenge to Israel in these passages:

> But if you fail to drive out the people who live in the land, those who remain will be like splinters in your eyes and thorns in your sides. They will harass you in the land where you live. (Numbers 33:55 NLT)

> So be very careful to love the Lord your God. But if you turn away from Him and cling to the customs of the survivors of these nations remaining among you, and if you intermarry with them, then know for certain that the Lord your God will no longer drive them out of your land. *Instead, they will be a snare and a trap to you, a whip for your backs and thorny brambles in your eyes,* and you will vanish from this good land the Lord your God has given you. (Joshua 23:11–13 NLT)

For your part, you were not to make any covenants with the people living in this land; instead, you were to destroy their altars. But you disobeyed my command. Why did you do this? So now I declare that I will no longer drive out the people living in your land. *They will be thorns in your sides, and their gods will be a constant temptation to you.* (Judges 2:2–3 NLT)

So, just as Israel was hindered by adopting some of the practices and ways of the pagan nations surrounding them, we too adopt many of the dysfunctions that are in our homes and families as children. These ways of doing life become our personal belief system.

Let's look at this a little more closely and examine how mind renewal and meditation can change wrong thinking in our personal belief system.

1. Our underlying thought patterns, our values, or our personal belief systems, rule how we live.

The following scripture is referring to our personal belief system. It is referring to the personal, internal set of rules we unconsciously use to live life and make decisions:

For if our heart condemns us, God is greater than our heart, and knows all things. Beloved, if our heart does not condemn us, we have confidence toward God. And whatever we ask we receive from Him, because we keep His commandments and do those things that are pleasing in His sight. (1 John 3:20–22 NKJV)

Whenever our hearts make us feel guilty and remind us of our failures, we know that God is much greater and more merciful than our conscience, and He knows everything there is to know about us. My delightfully loved friends, when our hearts don't condemn us, we have a bold freedom to speak face-to-face with God. (1 John 3:20–21 TPT)

Our conscience, our personal values system, or you could again call it our personal belief system, can condemn us when God is not condemning us. This system of underlying thoughts must be retrained so that our subconscious thinking is in line with what God says about life in general. And that is where mind renewal and meditation come into play.

The apostle Paul mentions the *spirit of your mind* in the book of Ephesians. The spirit of your mind is your personal belief system, or your conscience.

That you put off, concerning your former conduct, the old man which grows corrupt according to the deceitful lusts, and be renewed in the spirit of your mind, and that you put on the new man which was created according to God, in true righteousness and holiness. (Ephesians 4:22–24 NKJV)

The new birth affects our spirit nature. We become *new creatures in Christ* (2 Corinthians 5:17 NKJV). But our thoughts are minimally affected by the new birth. Our thoughts, both conscious thoughts and underlying patterns of thinking, must be changed. We can be free in Christ yet still bound by old ways of living and thinking. That's the reason Paul tells us to put off the old man or old ways of living and put on the new man (the person on the inside who has been born again).

This put-off, put-on process will not happen unless our minds begin to change. Notice what Paul said in Colossians 3:

> But now is the time to get rid of anger, rage, malicious behavior, slander, and dirty language. Don't lie to each other, for you have stripped off your old sinful nature and all its wicked deeds. Put on your new nature, and be renewed as you learn to know your Creator and become like Him. (Colossians 3:8–10 NLT)

2. Most of our personal belief system comes from our home life as children.

I read that somewhere around 85 percent of our beliefs are firmly set by age six or so. That means we pick up how we think and live from our home environment. So the obvious question is, What was your home environment like, and what do you think and believe about yourself, God, and others? These kinds of thoughts are so deeply embedded within our thoughts that we do not recognize they are there. It takes God, His Word, the Holy Spirit, and sometimes loving friends to open our eyes to what we cannot see about ourselves.

You can see this principle of our belief system being formed within us at a young age in the book of Deuteronomy:

> Listen, O Israel! The Lord is our God, the Lord alone. And you must love the Lord your God with all your heart, all your soul, and all your strength. And you must commit yourselves wholeheartedly to these commands that I am giving you today. Repeat them again and again to your children. Talk about them when you are at home and when you are on the road, when you are going to bed and when you are getting up. Tie them to your hands and wear them on your forehead as reminders. Write them

on the doorposts of your house and on your gates. (Deuteronomy 6:4–9 NLT)

Notice here that God commanded His people to talk about Him to their children all day long. They were to hear about God and His principle of life from the time they got up until they went to bed. Why did God tell them to talk about Him in their homes? He told them to do this because children are in their formative years at home, and God wants His ideals to be engrafted into the way they think when they are young! The principle is to "train up a child in the way he should go, and when he is old he will not depart from it" (Proverbs 22:6 NKJV).

What we learned at home is what we are most familiar with and what comes naturally to us. It's our default setting on life and how we deal with it. This does not change without intentional effort.

You are most comfortable with what is most familiar to you. Some people *choose dysfunction* because it is *for them* the most comfortable, the easiest way to live. It's their default. They learned it at home. And without outside help, we are mostly blind to it. Our belief system makes up the very fabric of our consciousness and how we think.

The problem is that there are no perfect homes and families. We are all flawed, and all families carry a measure of dysfunction in some area. We often repeat the failures of our mothers and fathers and our families because home is where the heart is. Notice what God says about this tendency in Exodus 34:

> I lavish unfailing love to a thousand generations.
> I forgive iniquity, rebellion, and sin. But I do not
> excuse the guilty. I lay the sins of the parents upon
> their children and grandchildren; the entire family
> is affected—even children in the third and fourth
> generations. (Exodus 34:7 NLT)

You shall not bow down to them nor serve them. For I, the Lord your God, am a jealous God, visiting the iniquity of the fathers upon the children to the third and fourth generations of those who hate Me, but showing mercy to thousands, to those who love Me and keep My commandments. (Exodus 20:5–6 NKJV)

You shall not bow down to them nor serve them. For I, the Lord your God, am a jealous God, visiting the iniquity of the fathers upon the children to the third and fourth generations of those who hate Me, but showing mercy to thousands, to those who love Me and keep My commandments. (Deuteronomy 5:9–10 NKJV)

Perhaps now we can understand the importance of living the Christian life at home for our children to see. If we do not live what we believe at home, then we are not training our children, and we are not placing in them by *observation, association,* and *influence* the needed values for a healthy personal belief system or conscience.

3. What is your personal belief system background?

Below is a chart I have included by permission from Lifeway, Inc., from a workbook titled *Untangling Relationships.* All of us have a measure of dysfunction to overcome, and the process begins by recognizing what needs to be changed. What from the chart and paragraphs below has been a part of your life and needs to change?

INDIVIDUAL NEEDS: LOVE SECURITY WORTH PROTECTION PROVISION			
	ENVIRONMENT	**RESULTS**	**MOTIVATION**
Healthy Families	FUNCTIONAL FAMILY: The freedom to feel love, honesty, acceptance, safety, provision for needs, loving discipline.	SPIRTUAL, EMOTIONAL, RELATIONAL HEALTH: Love, anger, fear, laughter intimacy, willingness to take risks.	HEALTHY MOTIVES: Love, thankfulness, obedience out of gratitude.
Dysfunctional Families	DYSFUNCTIONAL FAMILY: (Alcoholism, drug abuse, eating disorders, etc.): Condemnation, rejection, destructive criticism, manipulation, neglect, abuse, unreality, denial.	CODEPENDENCY: Lack of objectivity, warped sense of responsibility, controlled / controlling, guilt, hurt and anger, lonliness.	COMPULSIVE MOTIVES: Avoid pain, far of rejection, fear or failure, gain a sense of worth, accomplish goals to approval.

Dysfunctional Families

Alcoholism, drug addiction, workaholism, divorce, eating disorders, sexual disorders, absent father, absent mother, neglect, verbal abuse, emotional abuse, physical abuse, sexual abuse, domineering father/passive mother, domineering mother/ passive father, condemnation, rejection, destructive criticism, manipulation, neglect, unreality, denial, lack of objectivity, warped sense of responsibility, control, guilt, hurt and anger, loneliness

Functional Families

Unconditional love, unconditional acceptance, forgiveness, laughter, time to work and play together, attention, fun, freedom to express emotions appropriately, sense of personal worth, compassion, comfort, honesty, freedom to have your own opinion and your own identity, objectivity, affirmation, friendship, appropriate responsibility, loving correction

4. We often can't see who we really are.

Again, someone has said that we see life through colored glasses. These are the colored glasses of our experiences that are so familiar to us that we can't see in us what others see. It's like the yellow safety glasses I use when trimming my grass with a Weed eater. When I wear them, everything I see has a yellow tint. And that is how life is through the lens we see it from. We've thought a particular way for so long that we don't see how defective our thinking and belief system really are!

It takes illumination from the Holy Spirit to see the things about us that we need to change. Notice these scriptures:

> Our iniquities, our secret heart and its sins [which we would so like to conceal even from ourselves], You have set in the [revealing] light of Your countenance. (Psalm 90:8 AMPC)

> God, I invite your searching gaze into my heart. Examine me through and through; find out everything that may be hidden within me. Put me to the test and sift through all my anxious cares. See if there is any path of pain I'm walking on, and lead me back to your glorious, everlasting ways—the path that brings me back to you. (Psalm 139:23–24 TPT)

My friend Chip Judd has said, "God wants to identify, challenge, and change any patterns of thought, belief, or behavior that are contrary to His will. Many of these patterns are so much a part of us that we can't see them without the revelation of God's Spirit and the help of other loving Christians."

5. God created you to be loved!

God placed humans in a spiritual incubator called a family when born, so that they could grow and learn how to live in an environment of love. Before sin entered the equation of human life in the Garden of Eden through Adam and Eve, God's original intention was that human life be nurtured in a loving and caring environment. We are created to grow and thrive in an atmosphere of love. Notice what Jesus said to a person who asked Him about the most important things in God's laws:

> "Teacher, which is the most important commandment in the law of Moses?" Jesus replied, "'You must love the LORD your God with all your heart, all your soul, and all your mind.' This is the first and greatest commandment. A second is equally important: 'Love your neighbor as yourself.' The entire law and all the demands of the prophets are based on these two commandments." (Matthew 22:36–40 NLT)

Our personal belief system develops in a healthy way in an environment where love is emphasized. In a healthy family environment, we should learn how to love God, how to love ourselves, and how to love others, who often are so different from us!

6. Without unconditional love, our personal belief system will be fear based.

There are at least three kinds of fears that most people wrestle with in life, because we come from imperfect homes with imperfect parents. We have a fear of God, a fear of others, and a fear of being exposed.

Adam and Eve experienced these fears in the Garden of Eden after they fell into sin:

> And they heard the sound of the Lord God walking
> in the garden in the cool of the day, and Adam and
> his wife hid themselves from the presence of the
> Lord God among the trees of the garden. Then the
> Lord God called to Adam and said to him, "Where
> are you?" So he said, "I heard Your voice in the
> garden, and I was afraid because I was naked; and I
> hid myself." (Genesis 3:8–10 NKJV)

Years ago, my ministry friend Jack Frost used to say that Adam and Eve built a relational house around themselves when they sinned. They put a roof up to keep God at a distance. They built walls of self-protection around themselves so they would not be exposed to others. They became afraid of God, afraid of others, and afraid to take the walls down and become close to others.

When we fear God, we become afraid to open our hearts up to Him and reveal and talk to Him about what really bothers us. We feel that we do not measure up to the expectations we think He has of us. And then we often take on a salvation-by-works mentality, and then we perform to please. We perform to please God, and we perform to please others and be accepted by them.

The fear of God's presence produced in me an idea that God loved me because He had to, not because He wanted to, and that fear kept me away from God in my early years. I thought that God loved me because He *had* to, because He is love and is required to love everyone. Then I read John 16:27, and being afraid of God left me!

> For the Father Himself [tenderly] loves you because
> you have loved Me and have believed that I came out
> from the Father. (John 16:27 AMPC)

The fear of others produced in me a perfectionistic pride that required so much of myself that I could not enjoy life. Everything had to be just right. My hair (when I had it) had to be in place at all times. My clothes had to be just a certain way, and I projected an attitude that I was strong and never needed anything. I lived behind a mask. I would say and do things that I thought would cause others to like me. All of this behavior was based on fear. And the root of it was pride.

The fear of exposure made me want to isolate and be an introvert. I did not want others to get too close. They might see what I was really like and reject me! The mindset I had was that if you really knew what I was like, then you would not like me. That moved me to be alone in my young years.

7. Getting acquainted with love will begin to reset your personal belief system.

When I found out that God loved me unconditionally and that He wanted to be with me, my life began to change dramatically. When I finally opened up myself to be loved by God and to accept love from others, my personal belief system began to be transformed. Fears that controlled me in my youth began to melt away. My introverted personality came alive. Now, I hardly meet a stranger. The colored glasses came off when God's love through His Word opened my heart to accept His thoughts about me.

The following is a mixture of a few translations of 1 Corinthians 13:4–8 (NKJV) that I have used over the years to keep my mind renewed and my personal belief system sharp regarding God's love that is in me. Read this often, very slowly, and watch God begin to melt away years of hardness.

As you read this, ask God to point out anything that you need to change. When He does, repent of it; that is, tell Him what you have done or not done and ask Him to help you do that particular part of love as described here. It's a life-transforming exercise!

1 Corinthians 13:4–7 (NKJV)

Let me describe love. It is slow to lose patience; love stays in difficult relationships with kindness, and it always looks for ways to be constructive. There is no envy in love. It is not possessive and never boils over with jealousy. Love makes no parade of itself; it never boasts, nor does it puff up with pride. Love is never arrogant and never puts himself/herself on display, because it is neither anxious to impress, nor does it cherish inflated ideas of his/her own importance. Love never gets irritated and is never resentful.

Love holds no grudges, and he/she keeps no record of evil done to him/her. Love refuses to be provoked and never harbors evil thoughts.

Love is not rude or grasping or overly sensitive, nor does love search for imperfections and faults in others. Love does not compile statistics of evil or gloat over the wickedness of other people. On the contrary, it is glad with all good men when truth prevails. Love celebrates what is real and not what is perverse or incomplete.

Love never does the graceless thing. Love has good manners and does not pursue selfish advantage. Love never insists on his/her own rights, never irritably loses his/her temper, and never nurses his/her wrath to keep it warm. Love is not touchy.

Love can stand any kind of treatment because there are no limits to his/her endurance, no end to his/her trust. Love bears up under anything; he/she perseveres in all circumstances. Love's first instinct is to believe in people. If you love someone, you will be loyal to him no matter what the cost. You will always believe in him, always expect the best in him, and always stand your ground in defending him. Love never regards anyone or anything as hopeless. Love keeps up hope in everything. Love's hope never fades.

Love keeps on keeping on! It trusts in God in every situation and expects God to act in all circumstances. Love goes on forever. Nothing can destroy love. Nothing can happen that can break love's spirit. In fact, it is the one thing that still stands when all else has fallen.

CHAPTER FIVE

MEDITATION SCRIPTURES

Meditation does for the mind and spirit what chewing your food does for your body. Meditation takes the Word of God and drops it down into your heart.

Look again at the definition for *meditate* from Strong's Exhaustive Concordance:

> Meditate
>
> To murmur (in pleasure or anger); by implication, to ponder:—imagine, mourn, mutter, roar, speak, study, talk, utter, commune, complain, declare, meditate, muse, pray.

Verses That Emphasize Placing the Word Deep within You

> So get rid of all the filth and evil in your lives, and humbly accept the word God has planted in your hearts, for it has the power to save your souls. (James 1:21 NLT)

For we have the living Word of God, which is full of energy, and it pierces more sharply than a two-edged sword. It will even penetrate to the very core of our being where soul and spirit, bone and marrow meet! It interprets and reveals the true thoughts and secret motives of our hearts. (Hebrews 4:12 TPT)

This Book of the Law shall not depart from your mouth, but you shall meditate in it day and night, that you may observe to do according to all that is written in it. For then you will make your way prosperous, and then you will have good success. (Joshua 1:8 NKJV)

The scriptures in this chapter are focusing on who we are in Christ. I've listed them in New King James and New Living Translation for clarity. The bolded subheadings show what the verse contains in New King James: "In Christ," "In Whom," and so on.

Make each scripture your own by making it a confession. For instance, "Father, I thank You that I am a new creature in Christ. Old things in my life have passed away, and behold, all things are become new!"

I suggest ten to fifteen minutes a day for meditation. Sit back and say the scripture over and over again. Then take one scripture a day, and when you have free mental time, say that one scripture over and over to yourself slowly.

Your life will slowly begin to change. Your personal belief system will be transformed!

In Christ

Yet God, in His grace, freely makes us right in His sight. He did this through Christ Jesus when He freed us from the penalty for our sins. (Romans 3:24 NLT)

So now there is no condemnation for those who belong to Christ Jesus. (Romans 8:1 NLT)

And because you belong to him, the power of the life-giving Spirit has freed you from the power of sin that leads to death. (Romans 8:2 NLT)

So we, being many, are one body in Christ, and individually members of one another. (Romans 12:5 NKJV)

I am writing to God's church in Corinth, to you who have been called by God to be His own holy people. He made you holy by means of Christ Jesus, just as He did for all people everywhere who call on the name of our Lord Jesus Christ, their Lord and ours. (1 Corinthians 1:2 NLT)

But of Him you are in Christ Jesus, who became for us wisdom from God—and righteousness and sanctification and redemption. (1 Corinthians 1:30 NKJV)

God has united you with Christ Jesus. For our benefit God made Him to be wisdom itself. Christ made us right with God; He made us pure and holy, and He freed us from sin. (1 Corinthians 1:30 NLT)

For as in Adam all die, even so in Christ all shall be made alive. (1 Corinthians 15:22 NKJV)

Just as everyone dies because we all belong to Adam, everyone who belongs to Christ will be given new life. (1 Corinthians 15:22 NLT)

Now He who establishes us with you in Christ and has anointed us is God, who also has sealed us and given us the Spirit in our hearts as a guarantee. (2 Corinthians 1:21–22 NKJV)

It is God who enables us, along with you, to stand firm for Christ. He has commissioned us, and He has identified us as his own by placing the Holy Spirit in our hearts as the first installment that guarantees everything He has promised us. (2 Corinthians 1:21–22 NLT)

Now thanks be to God who always leads us in triumph in Christ, and through us diffuses the fragrance of His knowledge in every place. (2 Corinthians 2:14 NKJV)

But thank God! He has made us his captives and continues to lead us along in Christ's triumphal procession. Now he uses us to spread the knowledge of Christ everywhere, like a sweet perfume. (2 Corinthians 2:14 NLT)

But their minds were blinded. For until this day the same veil remains unlifted in the reading of the Old Testament, because the veil is taken away in Christ. (2 Corinthians 3:14 NKJV)

But the people's minds were hardened, and to this day whenever the old covenant is being read, the same veil covers their minds so they cannot understand the truth. And this veil can be removed only by believing in Christ. (2 Corinthians 3:14 NLT)

Therefore, if anyone is in Christ, he is a new creation; old things have passed away; behold, all things have become new. (2 Corinthians 5:17 NKJV)

This means that anyone who belongs to Christ has become a new person. The old life is gone; a new life has begun! (2 Corinthians 5:17 NLT)

That is, that God was in Christ reconciling the world to Himself, not imputing their trespasses to them, and has committed to us the word of reconciliation. (2 Corinthians 5:19 NKJV)

For God was in Christ, reconciling the world to himself, no longer counting people's sins against them. And He gave us this wonderful message of reconciliation. (2 Corinthians 5:19 NLT)

And this occurred because of false brethren secretly brought in (who came in by stealth to spy out our liberty which we have in Christ Jesus, that they might bring us into bondage). (Galatians 2:4 NKJV)

Even that question came up only because of some so-called believers there—false ones, really—who were secretly brought in. They sneaked in to spy on us and take away the freedom we have in Christ Jesus. They wanted to enslave us and force us to follow their Jewish regulations. (Galatians 2:4 NLT)

For you are all sons of God through faith in Christ Jesus. (Galatians 3:26 NKJV)

For you are all children of God through faith in Christ Jesus. (Galatians 3:26 NLT)

There is neither Jew nor Greek, there is neither slave nor free, there is neither male nor female; for you are all one in Christ Jesus. (Galatians 3:28 NKJV)

There is no longer Jew or Gentile, slave or free, male and female. For you are all one in Christ Jesus. (Galatians 3:28 NLT)

For in Christ Jesus neither circumcision nor uncircumcision avails anything, but faith working through love. (Galatians 5:6 NKJV)

For when we place our faith in Christ Jesus, there is no benefit in being circumcised or being uncircumcised. What is important is faith expressing itself in love. (Galatians 5:6 NLT)

For in Christ Jesus neither circumcision nor uncircumcision avails anything, but a new creation. (Galatians 6:15 NKJV)

It doesn't matter whether we have been circumcised or not. What counts is whether we have been transformed into a new creation. (Galatians 6:15 NLT)

Blessed be the God and Father of our Lord Jesus Christ, who has blessed us with every spiritual blessing in the heavenly places in Christ. (Ephesians 1:3 NKJV)

All praise to God, the Father of our Lord Jesus Christ, who has blessed us with every spiritual blessing in the heavenly realms because we are united with Christ. (Ephesians 1:3 NLT)

That in the dispensation of the fullness of the times He might gather together in one all things in Christ, both which are in heaven and which are on earth—in Him. (Ephesians 1:10 NKJV)

And this is the plan: At the right time he will bring everything together under the authority of Christ—everything in heaven and on earth. (Ephesians 1:10 NLT)

And raised us up together, and made us sit together in the heavenly places in Christ Jesus. (Ephesians 2:6 NKJV)

For He raised us from the dead along with Christ and seated us with Him in the heavenly realms because we are united with Christ Jesus. (Ephesians 2:6 NLT)

For we are His workmanship, created in Christ Jesus for good works, which God prepared beforehand that we should walk in them. (Ephesians 2:10 NKJV)

For we are God's masterpiece. He has created us anew in Christ Jesus, so we can do the good things he planned for us long ago. (Ephesians 2:10 NLT)

But now in Christ Jesus you who once were far off have been brought near by the blood of Christ. (Ephesians 2:13 NKJV)

But now you have been united with Christ Jesus. Once you were far away from God, but now you have been brought near to him through the blood of Christ. (Ephesians 2:13 NLT)

That the Gentiles should be fellow heirs, of the same body, and partakers of His promise in Christ through the gospel. (Ephesians 3:6 NKJV)

And this is God's plan: Both Gentiles and Jews who believe the Good News share equally in the riches inherited by God's children. Both are part of the same body, and both enjoy the promise of blessings because they belong to Christ Jesus. (Ephesians 3:6 NLT)

Brethren, I do not count myself to have apprehended; but one thing I do, forgetting those things which are behind and reaching forward to those things which are ahead, I press toward the goal for the prize of the upward call of God in Christ Jesus. (Philippians 3:13–14 NKJV)

No, dear brothers and sisters, I have not achieved it, but I focus on this one thing: Forgetting the past and looking forward to what lies ahead, I press on to reach the end of the race and receive the heavenly prize for which God, through Christ Jesus, is calling us. (Philippians 3:13–14 NLT)

Him we preach, warning every man and teaching every man in all wisdom, that we may present every man perfect in Christ Jesus. (Colossians 1:28 NKJV)

So we tell others about Christ, warning everyone and teaching everyone with all the wisdom God has given us. We want to present them to God, perfect in their relationship to Christ. (Colossians 1:28 NLT)

For the Lord Himself will descend from heaven with a shout, with the voice of an archangel, and with the trumpet of God. And the dead in Christ will rise first. Then we who are alive and remain shall be caught up together with them in the clouds to meet the Lord in the air. And thus we shall always be with the Lord. (1 Thessalonians 4:16–17 NKJV)

For the Lord Himself will come down from heaven with a commanding shout, with the voice of the archangel, and with the trumpet call of God. First, the believers who have died will rise from their graves. Then, together with them, we who are still alive and remain on the earth will be caught up in the clouds to meet the Lord in the air. Then we will be with the Lord forever. (1 Thessalonians 4:16–17 NLT)

In everything give thanks; for this is the will of God in Christ Jesus for you. (1 Thessalonians 5:18 NKJV)

Be thankful in all circumstances, for this is God's will for you who belong to Christ Jesus. (1 Thessalonians 5:18 NLT)

And the grace of our Lord was exceedingly abundant, with faith and love which are in Christ Jesus. (1 Timothy 1:14 NKJV)

Oh, how generous and gracious our Lord was! He filled me with the faith and love that come from Christ Jesus. (1 Timothy 1:14 NLT)

Who has saved us and called us with a holy calling, not according to our works, but according to His own purpose and grace which was given to us in Christ Jesus before time began. (2 Timothy 1:9 NKJV)

For God saved us and called us to live a holy life. He did this, not because we deserved it, but because that was his plan from before the beginning of time—to show us his grace through Christ Jesus. (2 Timothy 1:9 NLT)

Hold fast the pattern of sound words which you have heard from me, in faith and love which are in Christ Jesus. (2 Timothy 1:13 NKJV)

Hold on to the pattern of wholesome teaching you learned from me—a pattern shaped by the faith and love that you have in Christ Jesus. (2 Timothy 1:13 NLT)

You therefore, my son, be strong in the grace that is in Christ Jesus. (2 Timothy 2:1 NKJV)

Timothy, my dear son, be strong through the grace that God gives you in Christ Jesus. (2 Timothy 2:1 NLT)

Therefore I endure all things for the sake of the elect, that they also may obtain the salvation which is in Christ Jesus with eternal glory. (2 Timothy 2:10 NKJV)

So I am willing to endure anything if it will bring salvation and eternal glory in Christ Jesus to those God has chosen. (2 Timothy 2:10 NLT)

And that from childhood you have known the Holy Scriptures, which are able to make you wise for salvation through faith which is in Christ Jesus. (2 Timothy 3:15 NKJV)

You have been taught the holy Scriptures from childhood, and they have given you the wisdom to receive the salvation that comes by trusting in Christ Jesus. (2 Timothy 3:15 NLT)

That the sharing of your faith may become effective by the acknowledgment of every good thing which is in you in Christ Jesus. (Philemon 1:6 NKJV)

And I am praying that you will put into action the generosity that comes from your faith as you understand and experience all the good things we have in Christ. (Philemon 1:6 NLT)

For if these things are yours and abound, you will be neither barren nor unfruitful in the knowledge of our Lord Jesus Christ. (2 Peter 1:8 NKJV)

The more you grow like this, the more productive and useful you will be in your knowledge of our Lord Jesus Christ. (2 Peter 1:8 NLT)

Whoever transgresses and does not abide in the doctrine of Christ does not have God. He who abides in the doctrine of Christ has both the Father and the Son. (2 John 1:9 NKJV)

Anyone who wanders away from this teaching has no relationship with God. But anyone who remains in the teaching of Christ has a relationship with both the Father and the Son. (2 John 1:9 NLT)

In Him

For in Him we live and move and have our being, as also some of your own poets have said, "For we are also His offspring." (Acts 17:28 NKJV)

For in Him we live and move and exist. As some of your own poets have said, "We are His offspring." (Acts 17:28 NLT)

In Him was life, and the life was the light of men. (John 1:4 NKJV)

The Word gave life to everything that was created, and his life brought light to everyone. (John 1:4 NLT)

That whoever believes in Him should not perish but have eternal life. For God so loved the world that He gave His only begotten Son, that whoever believes in Him should not perish but have everlasting life. (John 3:15–16 NKJV)

So that everyone who believes in him will have eternal life. For this is how God loved the world: He gave his one and only Son, so that everyone who believes in him will not perish but have eternal life. (John 3:15–16 NLT)

For all the promises of God in Him are Yes, and in Him Amen, to the glory of God through us. (2 Corinthians 1:20 NKJV)

For all of God's promises have been fulfilled in Christ with a resounding "Yes!" And through Christ, our "Amen" (which means "Yes") ascends to God for his glory. (2 Corinthians 1:20 NLT)

For He made Him who knew no sin to be sin for us, that we might become the righteousness of God in Him. (2 Corinthians 5:21 NKJV)

For God made Christ, who never sinned, to be the offering for our sin, so that we could be made right with God through Christ. (2 Corinthians 5:21 NLT)

Just as He chose us in Him before the foundation of the world, that we should be holy and without blame before Him in love. (Ephesians 1:4 NKJV)

Even before He made the world, God loved us and chose us in Christ to be holy and without fault in His eyes. (Ephesians 1:4 NLT)

And be found in Him, not having my own righteousness, which is from the law, but that which is through faith in Christ, the righteousness which is from God by faith. (Philippians 3:9 NKJV)

And become one with Him. I no longer count on my own righteousness through obeying the law; rather, I become righteous through faith in Christ. For God's way of making us right with Himself depends on faith. (Philippians 3:9 NLT)

As you therefore have received Christ Jesus the Lord, so walk in Him, rooted and built up in Him and established in the faith, as you have been taught, abounding in it with thanksgiving. (Colossians 2:6–7 NKJV)

And now, just as you accepted Christ Jesus as your Lord, you must continue to follow Him. Let your roots grow down into Him, and let your lives be built on Him. Then your faith will grow strong in the truth you were taught, and you will overflow with thankfulness. (Colossians 2:6–7 NLT)

And you are complete in Him, who is the head of all principality and power. (Colossians 2:10 NKJV)

So you also are complete through your union with Christ, who is the head over every ruler and authority. (Colossians 2:10 NLT)

But whoever keeps His word, truly the love of God is perfected in him. By this we know that we are in Him. He who says he abides in Him ought himself also to walk just as He walked. (1 John 2:5–6 NKJV)

But those who obey God's word truly show how completely they love Him. That is how we know we are living in Him. Those who say they live in God should live their lives as Jesus did. (1 John 2:5–6 NLT)

Again, a new commandment I write to you, which thing is true in Him and in you, because the darkness is passing away, and the true light is already shining. (1 John 2:8 NKJV)

Yet it is also new. Jesus lived the truth of this commandment, and you also are living it. For the darkness is disappearing, and the true light is already shining. (1 John 2:8 NLT)

But the anointing which you have received from Him abides in you, and you do not need that anyone teach you; but as the same anointing teaches you concerning all things, and is true, and is not a lie, and just as it has taught you, you will abide in Him. And now, little children, abide in Him, that when He appears, we may have confidence and not be ashamed before Him at His coming. (1 John 2:27–28 NKJV)

But you have received the Holy Spirit, and he lives within you, so you don't need anyone to teach you what is true. For the Spirit teaches you everything you need to know, and what he teaches is true—it is not a lie. So just as he has taught you, remain in fellowship with Christ. And now, dear children, remain in fellowship with Christ so that when he returns, you will be full of courage and not shrink back from him in shame. (1 John 2:27–28 NLT)

And everyone who has this hope in Him purifies himself, just as He is pure. (1 John 3:3 NKJV)

And all who have this eager expectation will keep themselves pure, just as He is pure. (1 John 3:3 NLT)

And you know that He was manifested to take away our sins, and in Him there is no sin. Whoever abides in Him does not sin. Whoever sins has neither seen Him nor known Him. (1 John 3:5–6 NKJV)

And you know that Jesus came to take away our sins, and there is no sin in him. Anyone who continues to live in him will not sin. But anyone who keeps on sinning does not know him or understand who he is. (1 John 3:5–6 NLT)

Now he who keeps His commandments abides in Him, and He in him. And by this we know that He abides in us, by the Spirit whom He has given us. (1 John 3:24 NKJV)

Those who obey God's commandments remain in fellowship with Him, and He with them. And we know He lives in us because the Spirit He gave us lives in us. (1 John 3:24 NLT)

By this we know that we abide in Him, and He in us, because He has given us of His Spirit. (1 John 4:13 NKJV)

And God has given us His Spirit as proof that we live in Him and He in us. (1 John 4:13 NLT)

Now this is the confidence that we have in Him, that if we ask anything according to His will, He hears us. And if we know that He hears us, whatever we ask, we know that we have the petitions that we have asked of Him. (1 John 5:14–15 NKJV)

And we are confident that He hears us whenever we ask for anything that pleases Him. And since we know He hears us when we make our requests, we also know that He will give us what we ask for. (1 John 5:14–15 NLT)

And we know that the Son of God has come and has given us an understanding, that we may know Him who is true; and we are in Him who is true, in His Son Jesus Christ. This is the true God and eternal life. (1 John 5:20 NKJV)

And we know that the Son of God has come, and He has given us understanding so that we can know the true God. And now we live in fellowship with the true God because we live in fellowship with His Son, Jesus Christ. He is the only true God, and He is eternal life. (1 John 5:20 NLT)

In the Beloved

To the praise of the glory of His grace, by which He made us accepted in the Beloved. (Ephesians 1:6 NKJV)

So we praise God for the glorious grace he has poured out on us who belong to his dear Son. (Ephesians 1:6 NLT)

In the Lord

For you were once darkness, but now you are light in the Lord. Walk as children of light. (Ephesians 5:8 NKJV)

For once you were full of darkness, but now you have light from the Lord. So live as people of light! (Ephesians 5:8 NLT)

Finally, my brethren, be strong in the Lord and in the power of His might. (Ephesians 6:10 NKJV)

A final word: Be strong in the Lord and in His mighty power. (Ephesians 6:10 NLT)

In Whom

In Him we have redemption through His blood, the forgiveness of sins, according to the riches of His grace. (Ephesians 1:7 NKJV)

He is so rich in kindness and grace that He purchased our freedom with the blood of His Son and forgave our sins. (Ephesians 1:7 NLT)

In Him also we have obtained an inheritance, being predestined according to the purpose of Him who works all things according to the counsel of His will. (Ephesians 1:11 NKJV)

Furthermore, because we are united with Christ, we have received an inheritance from God, for He chose us in advance, and h\He makes everything work out according to His plan. (Ephesians 1:11 NLT)

In Him you also trusted, after you heard the word of truth, the gospel of your salvation; in whom also, having believed, you were sealed with the Holy Spirit of promise. (Ephesians 1:13 NKJV)

And now you Gentiles have also heard the truth, the Good News that God saves you. And when you believed in Christ, He identified you as His own by giving you the Holy Spirit, whom He promised long ago. (Ephesians 1:13 NLT)

In whom the whole building, being fitted together, grows into a holy temple in the Lord, in whom you also are being built together for a dwelling place of God in the Spirit. (Ephesians 2:21–22 NKJV)

In whom we have boldness and access with confidence through faith in Him. (Ephesians 3:12 NKJV)

Because of Christ and our faith in Him, we can now come boldly and confidently into God's presence. (Ephesians 3:12 NLT)

In whom we have redemption through His blood, the forgiveness of sins. (Colossians 1:14 NKJV)

Who purchased our freedom and forgave our sins. (Colossians 1:14 NLT)

In whom are hidden all the treasures of wisdom and knowledge. (Colossians 2:3 NKJV)

In Him lie hidden all the treasures of wisdom and knowledge. (Colossians 2:3 NLT)

In Him you were also circumcised with the circumcision made without hands, by putting off the body of the sins of the flesh, by the circumcision of Christ. (Colossians 2:11 NKJV)

When you came to Christ, you were "circumcised," but not by a physical procedure. Christ performed a spiritual circumcision—the cutting away of your sinful nature. (Colossians 2:11 NLT)

Whom having not seen you love. Though now you do not see Him, yet believing, you rejoice with joy inexpressible and full of glory. (1 Peter 1:8 NKJV)

You love Him even though you have never seen Him. Though you do not see Him now, you trust Him; and you rejoice with a glorious, inexpressible joy. (1 Peter 1:8 NLT)

By Christ

Even the righteousness of God, through faith in Jesus Christ, to all and on all who believe. For there is no difference. (Romans 3:22 NKJV)

We are made right with God by placing our faith in Jesus Christ. And this is true for everyone who believes, no matter who we are. (Romans 3:22 NLT)

But the free gift is not like the offense. For if by the one man's offense many died, much more the grace of God and the gift by the grace of the one Man, Jesus Christ, abounded to many. (Romans 5:15 NKJV)

But there is a great difference between Adam's sin and God's gracious gift. For the sin of this one man, Adam, brought death to many. But even greater is God's wonderful grace and his gift of forgiveness to many through this other man, Jesus Christ. (Romans 5:15 NLT)

For if by the one man's offense death reigned through the one, much more those who receive abundance of grace and of the gift of righteousness will reign in life through the One, Jesus Christ. Therefore, as through one man's offense judgment came to all men, resulting in condemnation, even so through one Man's righteous act the free gift came to all men, resulting in justification of life. For as by one man's disobedience many were made sinners, so also by one Man's obedience many will be made righteous. (Romans 5:17–19 NKJV)

For the sin of this one man, Adam, caused death to rule over many. But even greater is God's wonderful grace and His gift of righteousness, for all who receive it will live in triumph over sin and death through this one man, Jesus Christ. Yes, Adam's one sin brings condemnation for everyone, but Christ's one act of righteousness brings a right relationship with God and new life for everyone. Because one person disobeyed God, many became sinners. But because one other person obeyed God, many will be made righteous. (Romans 5:17–19 NLT)

Therefore, my brethren, you also have become dead to the law through the body of Christ, that you may be married to another—to Him who was raised from the dead, that we should bear fruit to God. (Romans 7:4 NKJV)

So, my dear brothers and sisters, this is the point: You died to the power of the law when you died with Christ. And now you are united with the One who was raised from the dead. As a result, we can produce a harvest of good deeds for God. (Romans 7:4 NLT)

I thank my God always concerning you for the grace of God which was given to you by Christ Jesus. (1 Corinthians 1:4 NKJV)

I always thank my God for you and for the gracious gifts he has given you, now that you belong to Christ Jesus. (1 Corinthians 1:4 NLT)

Now all things are of God, who has reconciled us to Himself through Jesus Christ, and has given us the ministry of reconciliation. (2 Corinthians 5:18 NKJV)

And all of this is a gift from God, who brought us back to Himself through Christ. And God has given us this task of reconciling people to Him. (2 Corinthians 5:18 NLT)

Knowing that a man is not justified by the works of the law but by faith in Jesus Christ, even we have believed in Christ Jesus, that we might be justified by faith in Christ and not by the works of the law; for by the works of the law no flesh shall be justified. (Galatians 2:16 NKJV)

Yet we know that a person is made right with God by faith in Jesus Christ, not by obeying the law. And we have believed in Christ Jesus, so that we might be made right with God because of our faith in Christ, not because we have obeyed the law. For no one will ever be made right with God by obeying the law. (Galatians 2:16 NLT)

Having predestined us to adoption as sons by Jesus Christ to Himself, according to the good pleasure of His will. (Ephesians 1:5 NKJV)

God decided in advance to adopt us into His own family by bringing us to Himself through Jesus Christ. This is what He wanted to do, and it gave Him great pleasure. (Ephesians 1:5 NLT)

Being filled with the fruits of righteousness which are by Jesus Christ, to the glory and praise of God. (Philippians 1:11 NKJV)

May you always be filled with the fruit of your salvation—the righteous character produced in your life by Jesus Christ—for this will bring much glory and praise to God. (Philippians 1:11 NLT)

And my God shall supply all your need according to His riches in glory by Christ Jesus. (Philippians 4:19 NKJV)

And this same God who takes care of me will supply all your needs from his glorious riches, which have been given to us in Christ Jesus. (Philippians 4:19 NLT)

Blessed be the God and Father of our Lord Jesus Christ, who according to His abundant mercy has begotten us again to a living hope through the resurrection of Jesus Christ from the dead. (1 Peter 1:3 NKJV)

All praise to God, the Father of our Lord Jesus Christ. It is by His great mercy that we have been born again, because God raised Jesus Christ from the dead. Now we live with great expectation. (1 Peter 1:3 NLT)

You also, as living stones, are being built up a spiritual house, a holy priesthood, to offer up spiritual sacrifices acceptable to God through Jesus Christ. (1 Peter 2:5 NKJV)

And you are living stones that God is building into his spiritual temple. What's more, you are his holy priests. Through the mediation of Jesus Christ, you offer spiritual sacrifices that please God. (1 Peter 2:5 NLT)

But may the God of all grace, who called us to His eternal glory by Christ Jesus, after you have suffered a while, perfect, establish, strengthen, and settle you. (1 Peter 5:10 NKJV)

In His kindness God called you to share in His eternal glory by means of Christ Jesus. So after you have suffered a little while, He will restore, support, and strengthen you, and He will place you on a firm foundation. (1 Peter 5:10 NLT)

That you were enriched in everything by Him in all utterance and all knowledge (1 Corinthians 1:5 NKJV)

Through Him, God has enriched your church in every way—with all of your eloquent words and all of your knowledge. (1 Corinthians 1:5 NLT)

Yet for us there is one God, the Father, of whom are all things, and we for Him; and one Lord Jesus Christ, through whom are all things, and through whom we live. (1 Corinthians 8:6 NKJV)

But for us, there is one God, the Father, by whom all things were created, and for Whom we live. And there is one Lord, Jesus Christ, through whom all things were created, and through Whom we live. (1 Corinthians 8:6 NLT)

For by Him all things were created that are in heaven and that are on earth, visible and invisible, whether thrones or dominions or principalities or powers. All things were created through Him and for Him. And He is before all things, and in Him all things consist. (Colossians 1:16–17 NKJV)

For through Him God created everything in the heavenly realms and on earth. He made the things we can see and the things we can't see—such as thrones, kingdoms, rulers, and authorities in the unseen world. Everything was created through Him and for Him. He existed before anything else, and

He holds all creation together. (Colossians 1:16–17 NLT)

And by Him to reconcile all things to Himself, by Him, whether things on earth or things in heaven, having made peace through the blood of His cross. (Colossians 1:20 NKJV)

And through him God reconciled everything to Himself. He made peace with everything in heaven and on earth by means of Christ's blood on the cross. (Colossians 1:20 NLT)

And whatever you do in word or deed, do all in the name of the Lord Jesus, giving thanks to God the Father through Him. (Colossians 3:17 NKJV)

And whatever you do or say, do it as a representative of the Lord Jesus, giving thanks through Him to God the Father. (Colossians 3:17 NLT)

Therefore He is also able to save to the uttermost those who come to God through Him, since He always lives to make intercession for them. (Hebrews 7:25 NKJV)

Therefore he is able, once and forever, to save those who come to God through Him. He lives forever to intercede with God on their behalf. (Hebrews 7:25 NLT)

Therefore by Him let us continually offer the sacrifice of praise to God, that is, the fruit of our lips, giving thanks to His name. (Hebrews 13:15 NKJV)

Therefore, let us offer through Jesus a continual sacrifice of praise to God, proclaiming our allegiance to His name. (Hebrews 13:15 NLT)

He indeed was foreordained before the foundation of the world, but was manifest in these last times for you who through Him believe in God, who raised Him from the dead and gave Him glory, so that your faith and hope are in God. (1 Peter 1:20–21 NKJV)

God chose Him as your ransom long before the world began, but now in these last days He has been revealed for your sake. Through Christ you have come to trust in God. And you have placed your faith and hope in God because he raised Christ from the dead and gave Him great glory. (1 Peter 1:20–21 NLT)

By Himself

Who being the brightness of His glory and the express image of His person, and upholding all things by the word of His power, when He had by Himself purged our sins, sat down at the right hand of the Majesty on high. (Hebrews 1:3 NKJV)

The Son radiates God's own glory and expresses the very character of God, and he sustains everything by the mighty power of his command. When He had cleansed us from our sins, He sat down in the place of honor at the right hand of the majestic God in heaven. (Hebrews 1:3 NLT)

He then would have had to suffer often since the foundation of the world; but now, once at the end of the ages, He has appeared to put away sin by the sacrifice of Himself. (Hebrews 9:26 NKJV)

If that had been necessary, Christ would have had to die again and again, ever since the world began. But now, once for all time, He has appeared at the end of the age to remove sin by His own death as a sacrifice. (Hebrews 9:26 NLT)

But Christ came as High Priest of the good things to come, with the greater and more perfect tabernacle not made with hands, that is, not of this creation. Not with the blood of goats and calves, but with His own blood He entered the Most Holy Place once for all, having obtained eternal redemption. (Hebrews 9:11–12 NKJV)

So Christ has now become the High Priest over all the good things that have come. He has entered that greater, more perfect Tabernacle in heaven, which was not made by human hands and is not part of this created world. With His own blood— not the blood of goats and calves—He entered the Most Holy Place once for all time and secured our redemption forever. (Hebrews 9:11–12 NLT)

How much more shall the blood of Christ, who through the eternal Spirit offered Himself without spot to God, cleanse your conscience from dead works to serve the living God? And for this reason He is the Mediator of the new covenant, by means of death, for the redemption of the transgressions under the first covenant, that those who are called may receive the promise of the eternal inheritance. (Hebrews 9:14–15 NKJV)

Just think how much more the blood of Christ will purify our consciences from sinful deeds so that we can worship the living God. For by the power of the eternal Spirit, Christ offered Himself to God as a perfect sacrifice for our sins. That is why He is the one who mediates a new covenant between God and people, so that all who are called can receive the eternal inheritance God has promised them. For Christ died to set them free from the penalty of the sins they had committed under that first covenant. (Hebrews 9:14–15 NLT)

Therefore, brethren, having boldness to enter the Holiest by the blood of Jesus, by a new and living way which He consecrated for us, through the veil, that is, His flesh. (Hebrews 10:19–20 NKJV)

And so, dear brothers and sisters, we can boldly enter heaven's Most Holy Place because of the blood of Jesus. By His death, Jesus opened a new and life-giving way through the curtain into the Most Holy Place. (Hebrews 10:19–20 NLT)

But if we walk in the light as He is in the light, we have fellowship with one another, and the blood of Jesus Christ His Son cleanses us from all sin. (1 John 1:7 NKJV)

But if we are living in the light, as God is in the light, then we have fellowship with each other, and the blood of Jesus, His Son, cleanses us from all sin. (1 John 1:7 NLT)

By Whom

Through whom also we have access by faith into this grace in which we stand, and rejoice in hope of the glory of God. (Romans 5:2 NKJV)

Because of our faith, Christ has brought us into this place of undeserved privilege where we now stand, and we confidently and joyfully look forward to sharing God's glory. (Romans 5:2 NLT)

And not only that, but we also rejoice in God through our Lord Jesus Christ, through whom we have now received the reconciliation. (Romans 5:11 NKJV)

So now we can rejoice in our wonderful new relationship with God because our Lord Jesus Christ has made us friends of God. (Romans 5:11 NLT)

But God forbid that I should boast except in the cross of our Lord Jesus Christ, by whom the world has been crucified to me, and I to the world. (Galatians 6:14 NKJV)

As for me, may I never boast about anything except the cross of our Lord Jesus Christ. Because of that cross, my interest in this world has been crucified, and the world's interest in me has also died. (Galatians 6:14 NLT)

From Whom

From whom the whole body, joined and knit together by what every joint supplies, according to the effective working by which every part does its share, causes growth of the body for the edifying of itself in love. (Ephesians 4:16 NKJV)

He makes the whole body fit together perfectly. As each part does its own special work, it helps the other parts grow, so that the whole body is healthy and growing and full of love. (Ephesians 4:16 NLT)

And not holding fast to the Head, from whom all the body, nourished and knit together by joints and ligaments, grows with the increase that is from God. (Colossians 2:19 NKJV)

And they are not connected to Christ, the head of the body. For He holds the whole body together with its joints and ligaments, and it grows as God nourishes it. (Colossians 2:19 NLT)

Of Christ

For we are to God the fragrance of Christ among those who are being saved and among those who are perishing. (2 Corinthians 2:15 NKJV)

Our lives are a Christ-like fragrance rising up to God. But this fragrance is perceived differently by those who are being saved and by those who are perishing. (2 Corinthians 2:15 NLT)

Not that I have already attained, or am already perfected; but I press on, that I may lay hold of that for which Christ Jesus has also laid hold of me. (Philippians 3:12 NKJV)

I don't mean to say that I have already achieved these things or that I have already reached perfection. But I press on to possess that perfection for which Christ Jesus first possessed me. (Philippians 3:12 NLT)

So let no one judge you in food or in drink, or regarding a festival or a new moon or sabbaths, which are a shadow of things to come, but the substance is of Christ. (Colossians 2:16–17 NKJV)

So don't let anyone condemn you for what you eat or drink, or for not celebrating certain holy days or new moon ceremonies or Sabbaths. For these rules are only shadows of the reality yet to come. And Christ himself is that reality. (Colossians 2:16–17 NLT)

Knowing that from the Lord you will receive the reward of the inheritance; for you serve the Lord Christ. (Colossians 3:24 NKJV)

Remember that the Lord will give you an inheritance as your reward, and that the Master you are serving is Christ. (Colossians 3:24 NLT)

Of Him

This is the message which we have heard from Him and declare to you, that God is light and in Him is no darkness at all. (1 John 1:5 NKJV)

This is the message we heard from Jesus and now declare to you: God is light, and there is no darkness in Him at all. (1 John 1:5 NLT)

Through Christ

Therefore, having been justified by faith, we have peace with God through our Lord Jesus Christ. (Romans 5:1 NKJV)

Therefore, since we have been made right in God's sight by faith, we have peace with God because of what Jesus Christ our Lord has done for us. (Romans 5:1 NLT)

And not only that, but we also rejoice in God through our Lord Jesus Christ, through whom we have now received the reconciliation. (Romans 5:11 NKJV)

So now we can rejoice in our wonderful new relationship with God because our Lord Jesus Christ has made us friends of God. (Romans 5:11 NLT)

Likewise you also, reckon yourselves to be dead indeed to sin, but alive to God in Christ Jesus our Lord. (Romans 6:11 NKJV)

So you also should consider yourselves to be dead to the power of sin and alive to God through Christ Jesus. (Romans 6:11 NLT)

For the wages of sin is death, but the gift of God is eternal life in Christ Jesus our Lord. (Romans 6:23 NKJV)

For the wages of sin is death, but the free gift of God is eternal life through Christ Jesus our Lord. (Romans 6:23 NLT)

But thanks be to God, who gives us the victory through our Lord Jesus Christ. (1 Corinthians 15:57 NKJV)

But thank God! He gives us victory over sin and death through our Lord Jesus Christ. (1 Corinthians 15:57 NLT)

Christ has redeemed us from the curse of the law, having become a curse for us (for it is written, "Cursed is everyone who hangs on a tree"), that the blessing of Abraham might come upon the Gentiles in Christ Jesus, that we might receive the promise of the Spirit through faith. (Galatians 3:13–14 NKJV)

But Christ has rescued us from the curse pronounced by the law. When He was hung on the cross, He took upon himself the curse for our wrongdoing. For it is written in the Scriptures, "Cursed is everyone who is hung on a tree." Through Christ Jesus, God has blessed the Gentiles with the same blessing he promised to Abraham, so that we who are believers might receive the promised Holy Spirit through faith. (Galatians 3:13–14 NLT)

Therefore you are no longer a slave but a son, and if a son, then an heir of God through Christ. (Galatians 4:7 NKJV)

Now you are no longer a slave but God's own child. And since you are His child, God has made you His heir. (Galatians 4:7 NLT)

That in the ages to come He might show the exceeding riches of His grace in His kindness toward us in Christ Jesus. (Ephesians 2:7 NKJV)

So God can point to us in all future ages as examples of the incredible wealth of His grace and kindness toward us, as shown in all He has done for us who are united with Christ Jesus. (Ephesians 2:7 NLT)

Be anxious for nothing, but in everything by prayer and supplication, with thanksgiving, let your requests be made known to God; and the peace of God, which surpasses all understanding, will guard your hearts and minds through Christ Jesus. (Philippians 4:6–7 NKJV)

Don't worry about anything; instead, pray about everything. Tell God what you need, and thank him for all he has done. Then you will experience God's peace, which exceeds anything we can understand. His peace will guard your hearts and minds as you live in Christ Jesus. (Philippians 4:6–7 NLT)

I can do all things through Christ who strengthens me. (Philippians 4:13 NKJV)

For I can do everything through Christ, who gives me strength. (Philippians 4:13 NLT)

By that will we have been sanctified through the offering of the body of Jesus Christ once for all. (Hebrews 10:10 NKJV)

For God's will was for us to be made holy by the sacrifice of the body of Jesus Christ, once for all time. (Hebrews 10:10 NLT)

Now may the God of peace who brought up our Lord Jesus from the dead, that great Shepherd of the sheep, through the blood of the everlasting covenant, make you complete in every good work to do His will, working in you what is well pleasing in His sight, through Jesus Christ, to whom be glory forever and ever. Amen. (Hebrews 13:20–21 NKJV)

Now may the God of peace—who brought up from the dead our Lord Jesus, the great Shepherd of the sheep, and ratified an eternal covenant with his blood—21 may He equip you with all you need for doing His will. May he produce in you, through the power of Jesus Christ, every good thing that is pleasing to Him. All glory to him forever and ever! Amen. (Hebrews 13:20–21 NLT)

Through Him

For God did not send His Son into the world to condemn the world, but that the world through Him might be saved. (John 3:17 NKJV)

God sent His Son into the world not to judge the world, but to save the world through Him. (John 3:17 NLT)

Much more then, having now been justified by His blood, we shall be saved from wrath through Him. (Romans 5:9 NKJV)

And since we have been made right in God's sight by the blood of Christ, He will certainly save us from God's condemnation. (Romans 5:9 NLT)

Yet in all these things we are more than conquerors through Him who loved us. (Romans 8:37 NKJV)

No, despite all these things, overwhelming victory is ours through Christ, Who loved us. (Romans 8:37 NLT)

In this the love of God was manifested toward us, that God has sent His only begotten Son into the world, that we might live through Him. (1 John 4:9 NKJV)

God showed how much He loved us by sending His one and only Son into the world so that we might have eternal life through Him. (1 John 4:9 NLT)

With Christ

Now if we died with Christ, we believe that we shall also live with Him. (Romans 6:8 NKJV)

And since we died with Christ, we know we will also live with Him. (Romans 6:8 NLT)

I have been crucified with Christ; it is no longer I who live, but Christ lives in me; and the life which I now live in the flesh I live by faith in the Son of God, who loved me and gave Himself for me. (Galatians 2:20 NKJV)

My old self has been crucified with Christ. It is no longer I who live, but Christ lives in me. So I live in this earthly body by trusting in the Son of God, who loved me and gave Himself for me. (Galatians 2:20 NLT)

Even when we were dead in trespasses, made us alive together with Christ (by grace you have been saved). (Ephesians 2:5 NKJV)

That even though we were dead because of our sins, He gave us life when He raised Christ from the dead. (It is only by God's grace that you have been saved!). (Ephesians 2:5 NLT)

Therefore, if you died with Christ from the basic principles of the world, why, as though living in the world, do you subject yourselves to regulations. (Colossians 2:20 NKJV)

You have died with Christ, and He has set you free from the spiritual powers of this world. So why do you keep on following the rules of the world. (Colossians 2:20 NLT)

If then you were raised with Christ, seek those things which are above, where Christ is, sitting at the right hand of God. (Colossians 3:1 NKJV)

Since you have been raised to new life with Christ, set your sights on the realities of heaven, where Christ sits in the place of honor at God's right hand. (Colossians 3:1 NLT)

For you died, and your life is hidden with Christ in God. (Colossians 3:3 NKJV)

For you died to this life, and your real life is hidden with Christ in God. (Colossians 3:3 NLT)

With Him

Therefore we were buried with Him through baptism into death, that just as Christ was raised from the dead by the glory of the Father, even so we also should walk in newness of life. (Romans 6:4 NKJV)

For we died and were buried with Christ by baptism. And just as Christ was raised from the dead by the glorious power of the Father, now we also may live new lives. (Romans 6:4 NLT)

Knowing this, that our old man was crucified with Him, that the body of sin might be done away with, that we should no longer be slaves of sin. (Romans 6:6 NKJV)

We know that our old sinful selves were crucified with Christ so that sin might lose its power in our lives. We are no longer slaves to sin. (Romans 6:6 NLT)

Now if we died with Christ, we believe that we shall also live with Him. (Romans 6:8 NKJV)

And since we died with Christ, we know we will also live with him. (Romans 6:8 NLT)

He who did not spare His own Son, but delivered Him up for us all, how shall He not with Him also freely give us all things? (Romans 8:32 NKJV)

Since He did not spare even His own Son but gave Him up for us all, won't He also give us everything else? (Romans 8:32 NLT)

For though He was crucified in weakness, yet He lives by the power of God. For we also are weak in Him, but we shall live with Him by the power of God toward you. (2 Corinthians 13:4 NKJV)

Although He was crucified in weakness, He now lives by the power of God. We, too, are weak, just as Christ was, but when we deal with you we will be alive with Him and will have God's power. (2 Corinthians 13:4 NLT)

Buried with Him in baptism, in which you also were raised with Him through faith in the working of God, who raised Him from the dead. (Colossians 2:12 NKJV)

For you were buried with Christ when you were baptized. And with him you were raised to new life because you trusted the mighty power of God, who raised Christ from the dead. (Colossians 2:12 NLT)

And you, being dead in your trespasses and the uncircumcision of your flesh, He has made alive together with Him, having forgiven you all trespasses, having wiped out the handwriting of requirements that was against us, which was contrary to us. And He has taken it out of the way, having nailed it to the cross. Having disarmed principalities and powers, He made a public spectacle of them, triumphing over them in it. (Colossians 2:13–15 NKJV)

You were dead because of your sins and because your sinful nature was not yet cut away. Then God made you alive with Christ, for He forgave all our sins. He canceled the record of the charges against us and took it away by nailing it to the cross. In this way, He disarmed the spiritual rulers and authorities. He shamed them publicly by His victory over them on the cross. (Colossians 2:13–15 NLT)

When Christ who is our life appears, then you also will appear with Him in glory. (Colossians 3:4 NKJV)

And when Christ, who is your life, is revealed to the whole world, you will share in all His glory. (Colossians 3:4 NLT)

This is a faithful saying: For if we died with Him, we shall also live with Him. If we endure, we shall also reign with Him. If we deny Him, He also will deny us. (2 Timothy 2:11–12 NKJV)

This is a trustworthy saying: If we die with Him, we will also live with Him. If we endure hardship, we will reign with Him. If we deny Him, He will deny us. (2 Timothy 2:11–12 NLT)

By Me

As the living Father sent Me, and I live because of the Father, so he who feeds on Me will live because of Me. (John 6:57 NKJV)

I live because of the living Father who sent Me; in the same way, anyone who feeds on Me will live because of Me. (John 6:57 NLT)

Jesus said to him, "I am the way, the truth, and the life. No one comes to the Father except through Me." (John 14:6 NKJV)

Jesus told him, "I am the way, the truth, and the life. No one can come to the Father except through Me." (John 14:6 NLT)

In Me

He who eats My flesh and drinks My blood abides in Me, and I in him. (John 6:56 NKJV)

Anyone who eats My flesh and drinks My blood remains in Me, and I in him. (John 6:56 NLT)

At that day you will know that I am in My Father, and you in Me, and I in you. (John 14:20 NKJV)

When I am raised to life again, you will know that I am in My Father, and you are in Me, and I am in you. (John 14:20 NLT)

Abide in Me, and I in you. As the branch cannot bear fruit of itself, unless it abides in the vine, neither can you, unless you abide in Me. "I am the vine, you are the branches. He who abides in Me, and I in him, bears much fruit; for without Me you can do nothing." (John 15:4–5 NKJV)

Remain in Me, and I will remain in you. For a branch cannot produce fruit if it is severed from the vine, and you cannot be fruitful unless you remain in Me. "Yes, I am the vine; you are the branches. Those who remain in Me, and I in them, will produce much fruit. For apart from Me you can do nothing. (John 15:4–5 NLT)

If you abide in Me, and My words abide in you, you will ask what you desire, and it shall be done for you. By this My Father is glorified, that you bear much fruit; so you will be My disciples. (John 15:7–8 NKJV)

But if you remain in Me and My words remain in you, you may ask for anything you want, and it will be granted! When you produce much fruit, you are My true disciples. This brings great glory to My Father. (John 15:7–8 NLT)

These things I have spoken to you, that in Me you may have peace. In the world you will have tribulation; but be of good cheer, I have overcome the world. (John 16:33 NKJV)

I have told you all this so that you may have peace in Me. Here on earth you will have many trials and sorrows. But take heart, because I have overcome the world. (John 16:33 NLT)

In My Love

As the Father loved Me, I also have loved you; abide in My love. (John 15:9 NKJV)

I have loved you even as the Father has loved Me. Remain in My love. (John 15:9 NLT)

In His Name

For where two or three are gathered together in My name, I am there in the midst of them. (Matthew 18:20 NKJV)

For where two or three gather together as My followers, I am there among them. (Matthew 18:20 NLT)

And these signs will follow those who believe: In My name they will cast out demons; they will speak with new tongues; they will take up serpents; and if they drink anything deadly, it will by no means hurt them; they will lay hands on the sick, and they will recover. (Mark 16:17–18 NKJV)

These miraculous signs will accompany those who believe: They will cast out demons in My name, and they will speak in new languages. They will be able to handle snakes with safety, and if they drink anything poisonous, it won't hurt them. They will be able to place their hands on the sick, and they will be healed. (Mark 16:17–18 NLT)

And whatever you ask in My name, that I will do, that the Father may be glorified in the Son. If you ask anything in My name, I will do it. (John 14:13–14 NKJV)

You can ask for anything in My name, and I will do it, so that the Son can bring glory to the Father. Yes, ask me for anything in My name, and I will do it! (John 14:13–14 NLT)

And in that day you will ask Me nothing. Most assuredly, I say to you, whatever you ask the Father in My name He will give you. Until now you have asked nothing in My name. Ask, and you will receive, that your joy may be full. (John 16:23–24 NKJV)

At that time you won't need to ask me for anything. I tell you the truth, you will ask the Father directly, and he will grant your request because you use my name. You haven't done this before. Ask, using my name, and you will receive, and you will have abundant joy. (John 16:23–24 NLT)

And such were some of you. But you were washed, but you were sanctified, but you were justified in the name of the Lord Jesus and by the Spirit of our God. (1 Corinthians 6:11 NKJV)

Some of you were once like that. But you were cleansed; you were made holy; you were made right with God by calling on the name of the Lord Jesus Christ and by the Spirit of our God. (1 Corinthians 6:11 NLT)

What You Have as a Believer in Christ

That it might be fulfilled which was spoken by Isaiah the prophet, saying: He Himself took our infirmities and bore our sicknesses. (Matthew 8:17 NKJV)

This fulfilled the word of the Lord through the prophet Isaiah, who said, He took our sicknesses and removed our diseases. (Matthew 8:17 NLT)

Come to Me, all you who labor and are heavy laden, and I will give you rest. Take My yoke upon you and learn from Me, for I am gentle and lowly in heart, and you will find rest for your souls. For My yoke is easy and My burden is light. (Matthew 11:28–30 NKJV)

Then Jesus said, Come to Me, all of you who are weary and carry heavy burdens, and I will give you rest. Take My yoke upon you. Let Me teach you, because I am humble and gentle at heart, and you will find rest for your souls. For my yoke is easy to bear, and the burden I give you is light. (Matthew 11:28–30 NLT)

For the Son of Man has come to save that which was lost. (Matthew 18:11 NKJV)

Assuredly, I say to you, whatever you bind on earth will be bound in heaven, and whatever you loose on earth will be loosed in heaven. "Again I say to you that if two of you agree on earth concerning anything that they ask, it will be done for them by My Father in heaven. For where two or three are gathered together in My name, I am there in the midst of them." (Matthew 18:18–20 NKJV)

I tell you the truth, whatever you forbid on earth will be forbidden in heaven, and whatever you permit on earth will be permitted in heaven. "I also tell you this: If two of you agree here on earth concerning anything you ask, My Father in heaven will do it for you. For where two or three gather together as My followers, I am there among them." (Matthew 18:18–20 NLT)

And Jesus came and spoke to them, saying, All authority has been given to Me in heaven and on earth. Go therefore and make disciples of all the nations, baptizing them in the name of the Father and of the Son and of the Holy Spirit, teaching them to observe all things that I have commanded you; and lo, I am with you always, even to the end of the age. Amen. (Matthew 28:18–20 NKJV)

Mitch Horton

Jesus came and told His disciples, I have been given all authority in heaven and on earth. Therefore, go and make disciples of all the nations, baptizing them in the name of the Father and the Son and the Holy Spirit. Teach these new disciples to obey all the commands I have given you. And be sure of this: I am with you always, even to the end of the age. (Matthew 28:18–20 NLT)

Jesus said to him, If you can believe, all things are possible to him who believes. (Mark 9:23 NKJV)

"What do you mean, If I can?" Jesus asked. "Anything is possible if a person believes." (Mark 9:23 NLT)

For assuredly, I say to you, whoever says to this mountain, "Be removed and be cast into the sea," and does not doubt in his heart, but believes that those things he says will be done, he will have whatever he says. Therefore I say to you, whatever things you ask when you pray, believe that you receive them, and you will have them. (Mark 11:23–24 NKJV)

I tell you the truth, you can say to this mountain, "May you be lifted up and thrown into the sea," and it will happen. But you must really believe it will happen and have no doubt in your heart. I tell you, you can pray for anything, and if you believe that you've received it, it will be yours. (Mark 11:23–24 NLT)

Behold, I give you the authority to trample on serpents and scorpions, and over all the power of the enemy, and nothing shall by any means hurt you. (Luke 10:19 NKJV)

Look, I have given you authority over all the power of the enemy, and you can walk among snakes and scorpions and crush them. Nothing will injure you. (Luke 10:19 NLT)

But whoever drinks of the water that I shall give him will never thirst. But the water that I shall give him will become in him a fountain of water springing up into everlasting life. (John 4:14 NKJV)

But those who drink the water I give will never be thirsty again. It becomes a fresh, bubbling spring within them, giving them eternal life. (John 4:14 NLT)

And this is the will of Him who sent Me, that everyone who sees the Son and believes in Him may have everlasting life; and I will raise him up at the last day. (John 6:40 NKJV)

For it is My Father's will that all who see His Son and believe in Him should have eternal life. I will raise them up at the last day. (John 6:40 NLT)

The thief does not come except to steal, and to kill, and to destroy. I have come that they may have life, and that they may have it more abundantly. (John 10:10 NKJV)

The thief's purpose is to steal and kill and destroy. My purpose is to give them a rich and satisfying life. (John 10:10 NLT)

Most assuredly, I say to you, he who believes in Me, the works that I do he will do also; and greater works than these he will do, because I go to My Father. (John 14:12 NKJV)

I tell you the truth, anyone who believes in Me will do the same works I have done, and even greater works, because I am going to be with the Father. (John 14:12 NLT)

Jesus answered and said to him, "If anyone loves Me, he will keep My word; and My Father will love him, and We will come to him and make Our home with him." (John 14:23 NKJV)

Jesus replied, "All who love Me will do what I say. My Father will love them, and We will come and make our home with each of them." (John 14:23 NLT)

I in them, and You in Me; that they may be made perfect in one, and that the world may know that You have sent Me, and have loved them as You have loved Me. (John 17:23 NKJV)

I am in them and you are in Me. May they experience such perfect unity that the world will know that You sent Me and that you love them as much as you love Me. (John 17:23 NLT)

And if you are Christ's, then you are Abraham's seed, and heirs according to the promise. (Galatians 3:29 NKJV)

And now that you belong to Christ, you are the true children of Abraham. You are His heirs, and God's promise to Abraham belongs to you. (Galatians 3:29 NLT)

Stand fast therefore in the liberty by which Christ has made us free, and do not be entangled again with a yoke of bondage. (Galatians 5:1 NKJV)

So Christ has truly set us free. Now make sure that you stay free, and don't get tied up again in slavery to the law. (Galatians 5:1 NLT)

Let this mind be in you which was also in Christ Jesus (Philippians 2:5 NKJV)

You must have the same attitude that Christ Jesus had. (Philippians 2:5 NLT)

For it is God who works in you both to will and to do for His good pleasure. (Philippians 2:13 NKJV)

For God is working in you, giving you the desire and the power to do what pleases Him. (Philippians 2:13 NLT)

He has delivered us from the power of darkness and conveyed us into the kingdom of the Son of His love. (Colossians 1:13 NKJV)

For He has rescued us from the kingdom of darkness and transferred us into the Kingdom of His dear Son. (Colossians 1:13 NLT)

The mystery which has been hidden from ages and from generations, but now has been revealed to His saints. To them God willed to make known what are the riches of the glory of this mystery among the Gentiles: which is Christ in you, the hope of glory. (Colossians 1:26–27 NKJV)

This message was kept secret for centuries and generations past, but now it has been revealed to God's people. For God wanted them to know that the riches and glory of Christ are for you Gentiles, too. And this is the secret: Christ lives in you. This gives you assurance of sharing His glory. (Colossians 1:26–27 NLT)

Who gave Himself for us, that He might redeem us from every lawless deed and purify for Himself His own special people, zealous for good works. (Titus 2:14 NKJV)

He gave His life to free us from every kind of sin, to cleanse us, and to make us His very own people, totally committed to doing good deeds. (Titus 2:14 NLT)

That having been justified by His grace we should become heirs according to the hope of eternal life. (Titus 3:7 NKJV)

Because of His grace He made us right in His sight and gave us confidence that we will inherit eternal life. (Titus 3:7 NLT)

But we see Jesus, who was made a little lower than the angels, for the suffering of death crowned with glory and honor, that He, by the grace of God, might taste death for everyone. For it was fitting for Him, for whom are all things and by whom are all things, in bringing many sons to glory, to make the captain of their salvation perfect through sufferings. For both He who sanctifies and those who are being sanctified are all of one, for which reason He is not ashamed to call them brethren. (Hebrews 2:9–11 NKJV)

What we do see is Jesus, who for a little while was given a position "a little lower than the angels"; and because He suffered death for us, He is now "crowned with glory and honor." Yes, by God's grace, Jesus tasted death for everyone. God, for whom and through whom everything was made, chose to bring many children into glory. And it was only right that He should make Jesus, through his suffering, a perfect leader, fit to bring them into their salvation. So now Jesus and the ones He makes holy have the same Father. That is why Jesus is not ashamed to call them His brothers and sisters. (Hebrews 2:9–11 NLT)

Inasmuch then as the children have partaken of flesh and blood, He Himself likewise shared in the same, that through death He might destroy him who had the power of death, that is, the devil, and release those who through fear of death were all their lifetime subject to bondage. (Hebrews 2:14–15 NKJV)

Because God's children are human beings—made of flesh and blood—the Son also became flesh and blood. For only as a human being could He die, and only by dying could He break the power of the devil, who had the power of death. Only in this way could He set free all who have lived their lives as slaves to the fear of dying. (Hebrews 2:14–15 NLT)

For in that He Himself has suffered, being tempted, He is able to aid those who are tempted. (Hebrews 2:18 NKJV)

Since he Himself has gone through suffering and testing, He is able to help us when we are being tested. (Hebrews 2:18 NLT)

Seeing then that we have a great High Priest who has passed through the heavens, Jesus the Son of God, let us hold fast our confession. For we do not have a High Priest who cannot sympathize with our weaknesses, but was in all points tempted as we are, yet without sin. 16 Let us therefore come boldly to the throne of grace, that we may obtain mercy and find grace to help in time of need. (Hebrews 4:14–16 NKJV)

So then, since we have a great High Priest who has entered heaven, Jesus the Son of God, let us hold firmly to what we believe. This High Priest of ours understands our weaknesses, for He faced all of the same testings we do, yet He did not sin. So let us come boldly to the throne of our gracious God. There we will receive His mercy, and we will find grace to help us when we need it most. (Hebrews 4:14–16 NLT)

For the law made nothing perfect; on the other hand, there is the bringing in of a better hope, through which we draw near to God. (Hebrews 7:19 NKJV)

For the law never made anything perfect. But now we have confidence in a better hope, through which we draw near to God. (Hebrews 7:19 NLT)

By so much more Jesus has become a surety of a better covenant. (Hebrews 7:22 NKJV)

Because of this oath, Jesus is the one who guarantees this better covenant with God. (Hebrews 7:22 NLT)

But now He has obtained a more excellent ministry, inasmuch as He is also Mediator of a better covenant, which was established on better promises. (Hebrews 8:6 NKJV)

But now Jesus, our High Priest, has been given a ministry that is far superior to the old priesthood, for He is the one who mediates for us a far better covenant with God, based on better promises. (Hebrews 8:6 NLT)

For Christ has not entered the holy places made with hands, which are copies of the true, but into heaven itself, now to appear in the presence of God for us. (Hebrews 9:24 NKJV)

For Christ did not enter into a holy place made with human hands, which was only a copy of the true one in heaven. He entered into heaven itself to appear now before God on our behalf. (Hebrews 9:24 NLT)

So Christ was offered once to bear the sins of many. To those who eagerly wait for Him He will appear a second time, apart from sin, for salvation. (Hebrews 9:28 NKJV)

So also Christ was offered once for all time as a sacrifice to take away the sins of many people. He will come again, not to deal with our sins, but to bring salvation to all who are eagerly waiting for Him. (Hebrews 9:28 NLT)

For by one offering He has perfected forever those who are being sanctified. (Hebrews 10:14 NKJV)

For by that one offering He forever made perfect those who are being made holy. (Hebrews 10:14 NLT)

Let your conduct be without covetousness; be content with such things as you have. For He Himself has said, "I will never leave you nor forsake you." So we may boldly say: "The Lord is my helper; I will not fear. What can man do to me?" (Hebrews 13:5–6 NKJV)

Don't love money; be satisfied with what you have. For God has said, I will never fail you. I will never abandon you. So we can say with confidence, The Lord is my helper, so I will have no fear. What can mere people do to me? (Hebrews 13:5–6 NLT)

Jesus Christ is the same yesterday, today, and forever. (Hebrews 13:8 NKJV)

Jesus Christ is the same yesterday, today, and forever. (Hebrews 13:8 NLT)

Therefore submit to God. Resist the devil and he will flee from you. (James 4:7 NKJV)

So humble yourselves before God. Resist the devil, and he will flee from you. (James 4:7 NLT)

But you are a chosen generation, a royal priesthood, a holy nation, His own special people, that you may proclaim the praises of Him who called you out of darkness into His marvelous light. (1 Peter 2:9 NKJV)

But you are not like that, for you are a chosen people. You are royal priests, a holy nation, God's very own possession. As a result, you can show others the goodness of God, for He called you out of the darkness into his wonderful light. (1 Peter 2:9 NLT)

For to this you were called, because Christ also suffered for us, leaving us an example, that you should follow His steps. (1 Peter 2:21 NKJV)

For God called you to do good, even if it means suffering, just as Christ suffered for you. He is your example, and you must follow in His steps. (1 Peter 2:21 NLT)

For Christ also suffered once for sins, the just for the unjust, that He might bring us to God, being put to death in the flesh but made alive by the Spirit. (1 Peter 3:18 NKJV)

Christ suffered for our sins once for all time. He never sinned, but He died for sinners to bring you safely home to God. He suffered physical death, but he was raised to life in the Spirit. (1 Peter 3:18 NLT)

Casting all your care upon Him, for He cares for you. (1 Peter 5:7 NKJV)

Give all your worries and cares to God, for He cares about you. (1 Peter 5:7 NLT)

If we confess our sins, He is faithful and just to forgive us our sins and to cleanse us from all unrighteousness. (1 John 1:9 NKJV)

But if we confess our sins to Him, He is faithful and just to forgive us our sins and to cleanse us from all wickedness. (1 John 1:9 NLT)

My little children, these things I write to you, so that you may not sin. And if anyone sins, we have an Advocate with the Father, Jesus Christ the righteous. (1 John 2:1 NKJV)

My dear children, I am writing this to you so that you will not sin. But if anyone does sin, we have an advocate who pleads our case before the Father. He is Jesus Christ, the One who is truly righteous. (1 John 2:1 NLT)

Beloved, now we are children of God; and it has not yet been revealed what we shall be, but we know that when He is revealed, we shall be like Him, for we shall see Him as He is. (1 John 3:2 NKJV)

Dear friends, we are already God's children, but He has not yet shown us what we will be like when Christ appears. But we do know that we will be like Him, for we will see Him as He really is. (1 John 3:2 NLT)

We know that we have passed from death to life, because we love the brethren. He who does not love his brother abides in death. (1 John 3:14 NKJV)

If we love our brothers and sisters who are believers, it proves that we have passed from death to life. But a person who has no love is still dead. (1 John 3:14 NLT)

You are of God, little children, and have overcome them, because He who is in you is greater than he who is in the world. (1 John 4:4 NKJV)

But you belong to God, my dear children. You have already won a victory over those people, because the Spirit who lives in you is greater than the spirit who lives in the world. (1 John 4:4 NLT)

In this is love, not that we loved God, but that He loved us and sent His Son to be the propitiation for our sins. (1 John 4:10 NKJV)

This is real love—not that we loved God, but that He loved us and sent his Son as a sacrifice to take away our sins. (1 John 4:10 NLT)

Whoever confesses that Jesus is the Son of God, God abides in him, and he in God. (1 John 4:15 NKJV)

All who declare that Jesus is the Son of God have God living in them, and they live in God. (1 John 4:15 NLT)

Whoever believes that Jesus is the Christ is born of God, and everyone who loves Him who begot also loves him who is begotten of Him. (1 John 5:1 NKJV)

Everyone who believes that Jesus is the Christ has become a child of God. And everyone who loves the Father loves His children, too. (1 John 5:1 NLT)

For whatever is born of God overcomes the world. And this is the victory that has overcome the world—our faith. Who is he who overcomes the world, but he who believes that Jesus is the Son of God? (1 John 5:4–5 NKJV)

For every child of God defeats this evil world, and we achieve this victory through our faith. And who can win this battle against the world? Only those who believe that Jesus is the Son of God. (1 John 5:4–5 NLT)

And this is the testimony: that God has given us eternal life, and this life is in His Son. He who has the Son has life; he who does not have the Son of God does not have life. (1 John 5:11–12 NKJV)

And this is what God has testified: He has given us eternal life, and this life is in His Son. Whoever has the Son has life; whoever does not have God's Son does not have life. (1 John 5:11–12 NLT)

And from Jesus Christ, the faithful witness, the firstborn from the dead, and the ruler over the kings of the earth. To Him who loved us and washed us from our sins in His own blood, and has made us kings and priests to His God and Father, to Him be glory and dominion forever and ever. Amen. (Revelation 1:5–6 NKJV)

And from Jesus Christ. He is the faithful witness to these things, the first to rise from the dead, and the ruler of all the kings of the world. All glory to him who loves us and has freed us from our sins by shedding his blood for us. He has made us a Kingdom of priests for God his Father. All glory and power to him forever and ever! Amen. (Revelation 1:5–6 NLT)

CONCLUSION

My hope is that you have gleaned some helpful information from this book that will help you gain control of your thinking patterns and bring God's peace into your everyday life.

Many years ago, I developed a habit of rising early to spend devotional time with the Lord. During this time, I read my Bible, I read a chapter in a couple of books, and then I meditate for a few minutes on scripture before I pray. The dividends of this schedule for my personal life have been life transforming.

I would like to encourage you as well to begin your day with the Lord. You will find that as you direct your thoughts to Him at the beginning of your day, a pattern will evolve of learning to keep your thoughts on scripture throughout your day.

Take some time each day to take a few of the scriptures in the last chapter and read them slowly and quietly over and over. After a few days, you will begin to form a habit of meditating. Next year this time, you will not be the same person!

> Father, draw our hearts to you. May we find, as Job says, that your Word is more important than our needed daily food. (Job 23:12 NLT)

And may Isaiah 26:3 be fulfilled in every person who reads and practices the contents of this book. In Jesus's name.

> You will keep in perfect peace all who trust in You, all whose thoughts are fixed on You! (Isaiah 26:3 NLT)

ABOUT THE AUTHOR

Mitch Horton has been a Christian for more than forty-four years and brings a wealth of personal experience in this book. Mitch has been in Christian ministry since 1981 and has served on the pastoral team of Grace Church in Tulsa, Oklahoma, with Bob Yandian. He has also traveled and taught from church to church in his own ministry as well as serving as an associate pastor. Mitch has served as senior pastor of Victory Church in Raleigh, North Carolina, since 1994, where he currently leads Victory Church, a thriving congregation.

After attending a Bible school in his hometown, he graduated from Rhema Bible College in Tulsa, Oklahoma, in 1980. He earned a master of divinity degree from Christian Life School of Theology in Columbus, Georgia.

Mitch and his wife, Susan, have been married for more than forty-one years and have four children and soon-to-be eight grandchildren. He enjoys spending his leisure hours with his bustling family and cycling on his road bike on the Neuse River Greenway in Raleigh.

Printed in the United States
by Baker & Taylor Publisher Services